T0352035

The Cambridge Manuals of Science and
Literature

EXPERIMENTAL PSYCHOLOGY

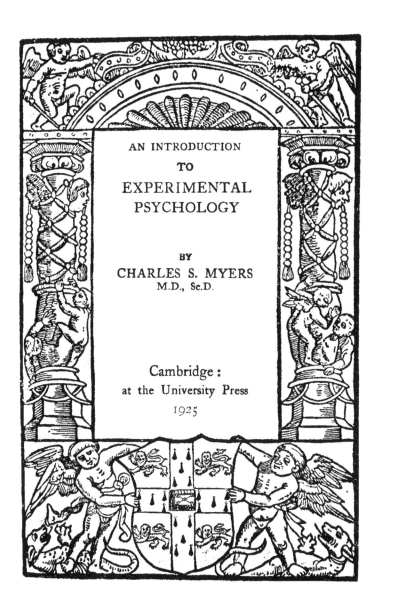

AN INTRODUCTION

TO

EXPERIMENTAL
PSYCHOLOGY

BY

CHARLES S. MYERS
M.D., Sc.D.

Cambridge:
at the University Press
1925

CAMBRIDGE UNIVERSITY PRESS
Cambridge, New York, Melbourne, Madrid, Cape Town,
Singapore, São Paulo, Delhi, Mexico City

Cambridge University Press
The Edinburgh Building, Cambridge CB2 8RU, UK

Published in the United States of America by Cambridge University Press, New York

www.cambridge.org
Information on this title: www.cambridge.org/9781107605800

© Cambridge University Press 1914

First Edition 1911.
Revised 1912.
Third Edition 1914.
Reprinted 1925
First paperback edition 2012

A catalogue record for this publication is available from the British Library

ISBN 978-1-107-60580-0 Paperback

*With the exception of the coat of arms at
the foot, the design on the title page is a
reproduction of one used by the earliest known
Cambridge printer, John Siberch, 1521*

PREFACE TO THIRD ISSUE

IN writing this little book, I have tried to keep in mind the purpose of the series to which it belongs. I have selected various topics which may fairly be considered typical themes of research in Experimental Psychology, and I have endeavoured to present them in such a form as will give the reader a general notion of the scope of the Science and of the experimental methods it employs.

A stranger to Experimental Psychology is almost certain at the outset to raise several objections. He may ask : Is not mind characterised by purpose and by a freedom from the mechanism that blindly controls the physical world? If so, how can mind be subject to experiment? Or, he may ask, how in any case is Experimental Psychology possible? Has the experimenter to cut up brains and nerves and to see what disturbances in behaviour will result? Or again, if only normal intact subjects are to be experimented upon, are not their minds so different

that it must be useless to apply to mankind as a
whole the results that have been obtained from one
or two individuals ?

That mind appears to be characterised by purpose
needs to be considered beside a similar statement
which is possible in regard to the universe.   Both
statements may rest only on superficial appearances,
or both may be true ; but it seems unlikely that one
of them is true while the other is false.   Now, even
if it be admitted that the history of the universe
cannot be satisfactorily described merely in terms of
mechanism and chance, nevertheless a Science is still
possible, not only of the lifeless but also of the living
world.   Physiological experiment is not necessarily
forbidden ground for the scientific worker who
realises the philosophical limitations of mechanism.
Nor is the similarly situated Psychologist debarred
from psychological experiment.   All that must be
admitted as fundamental for a Scientific Psychology
is that the same conditions must inevitably produce
the same results : so that if at any moment we know
all the conditions acting upon (or within) the mind
of an individual, and if we have had previous knowledge of their results, we can predict the state of
mind and the outward behaviour or conduct of that
individual at that moment.

The subject-matter of Psychology may be broadly
ranged under (i) mental acts (or processes) and

(ii) the mental contents (or products) that result from (i). The Self may or may not be conscious of mental acts ; compare, for example, the act of attending to a story or of recalling a name with the act of sensing blue or of perceiving a quite familiar object. Clearly too, the Self may or may not be conscious of mental contents or products ; the so-called sub-conscious experience abounds with mental products of which the Self is unconscious. Experimental Psychology has only of late years begun to investigate the 'highest' mental acts and contents such as those of thinking and of willing ; yet it has already reaped a promising harvest in these fields. During its relatively short existence its energies have been for the most part directed to the 'lower' acts and contents, especially to those concerned with sensation, perception and memory. Here it proceeds in close union with Physiology, the one occupied with the analysis and inter-relation of mental processes, the other with the determination and localisation of the functions of nervous matter.

The first two chapters of this book illustrate the close relation between Psychological and Physiological Experiment. They show what great help physiological experiment and pathological observations may give to ultimate psychological analysis. But they also show that our physiological knowledge of the higher nervous system is far behind our psychological knowledge of the corresponding mental processes and products. We know, for example, that the retinal cones are stimulated when we experience sensations of light and colour with bright illumination ; we know that the retinal rods are stimulated when we experience colourless sensations in dim light (Chapter I). But we know nothing as to the physiological basis of our different sensations of colour ; we do not know whether each cone contains within itself different apparatus each of which reacts to a different colour stimulus ; we do not know how far the various visual sensations are due to retinal, how far to cerebral physiological processes. So, too, although we know that under appropriate physiological or pathological conditions very different systems of cutaneous sensibility are revealed (Chapter II), we are quite ignorant of the physiological basis of such differences : we do not know whether, for example, there are quite different nervous paths for each of the two systems.

In the case of memory (Chapter V), the independent and unequal progress of psychology and neuro-physiology is still further manifest. The psychological facts, revealed by experiment on memory, stand absolutely without corresponding physiological knowledge. Physiological hypotheses, of course, abound to 'explain' the ascertained psychological facts, but as yet we *know* nothing even of so elementary a subject as the nature of the changes left behind in nervous tissue by a preceding excitation. We talk glibly of 'facilitation' and 'inhibition' in memory, attention, practice and fatigue; but we have no knowledge of the nature of these processes, and so far they have only proved capable of physiological study in the lowest regions of the central nervous system. We do not know whether there are cerebral 'centres' for memory, apart from cerebral 'centres' for perception; indeed, the physiologist's former conception of centres as 'seats' of conscious processes is now being seriously called in question. As psychological science has advanced, more careful pathological examinations have been prompted, with the result that most of the previously accepted facts of cerebral localisation are shown to be hypotheses based on insufficient neurological observation under the dominance of a contemporary but now antiquated psychology.

The fact that individual minds differ *inter se* is no barrier, but rather an incentive to psychological experiment. It is precisely the investigation of individual mental differences which has enabled experiment to give so great an impetus to the older psychology. Psychologists were once apt to imagine that all minds were like their own, and the 'general' psychologies they each constructed from self-introspection suffered accordingly. It is of course always open to Psychology to busy itself with the *average* characteristics, the *average* thresholds, the *average* imagery, the *average* memory, etc., of the human or animal mind. But the special interest of Psychology surely lies in the investigation of mental *differences*— the *differences* between the human and the animal minds, the *differences* between minds of the same genus, human or animal, the *differences* between minds of various species or races, the *differences* between abnormally brilliant, normal, and abnormally dull or defective minds.

Such differences can only be reliably ascertained by the use of experimental methods, the sole purpose of which is to specify as clearly as possible the conditions under which the psychological facts observed have been obtained. The conditions of a psychological experiment are clearly of two kinds : the internal conditions obtaining in the individual who is subjected to the experiment, and the external conditions of the experiment which is performed upon him. Both sets of conditions may be varied according to the wish of the experimenter in different experiments ; thus the subject may be examined in different internal conditions, e.g. of fatigue, practice, attention, knowledge as to the object of the experiment, etc. The external conditions may also be varied, provided that steps be taken from the outset to regulate the methods of conducting the experiment. For this purpose definite psycho-physical methods have been devised and recognised, the adoption or neglect of which at once distinguishes the trained from the untrained worker in Experimental Psychology.

No amount of reading, no amount of apparatus, only repeated practice with the simplest material, can give the requisite familiarity with the various uses and advantages of the different psycho-physical methods. The three important methods are (i) the limiting method, also called the method of least perceptible difference or the method of minimal changes ; (ii) the constant method, also called the method of right and wrong cases ; (iii) the method of mean error, also called the method of production. In this little book the use of the method of serial groups (a modification of the limiting method) is described on pages 21, 91, 97 and 99 ff. ; the constant method is described on pages 45 ff. ; the method of mean error is described on page 55[1].

It must be remembered that the value of a close acquaintance with the psycho-physical methods is not confined to the field of 'pure' Experimental Psychology, but that it extends to all investigations on the mind whenever observations are required under prescribed conditions which may be repeated later by the same or by different experimenters on

[1] The student who desires a more adequate knowledge of the subject, and of the use of statistical methods and formulae, must consult some larger work, e.g. my *Text-book of Experimental Psychology*.

the same or on different subjects, or which may be expressly modified later by the same or by different experimenters ; for example, in 'applied' psychological research on problems in Education, Aesthetics, Ethnology, or Sociology.

C. S. M.

CAMBRIDGE, 1914

CONTENTS

*** The apparatus described in this book can be obtained through the Attendant of the Cambridge Psychological Laboratory at approximately the following charges :

	£	s.	d.	
Tintometer and Glasses (p. 21)	4	0	0	
Rods for demonstrating Cold Spots (p. 33)...		3	0	per doz.
Pointed Bar (aluminium) for demonstrating Heat Spots (p. 33)		6	0	each
Compasses for Spatial Threshold (pp. 35, 99)		2	0	each
Müller-Lyer Illusion (p. 55)	1	5	0	
Memory Apparatus (p. 78)	1	0	0	
E Test for Visual Acuity (p. 92) ...		1	0	
Tuning Forks for Pitch Discrimination (p. 95)...	1	15	0	per pair
Calculating Test (p. 112)...		4	6	per 360 sheets
Letter-erasing Test (p. 118)		4	0	per 350 sheets
Stop Watch (p. 120)		15	0	

*** With the exception of five of the figures which have been taken from my *Text-book of Experimental Psychology*, and two (figs. 5 and 20) which are borrowed from the *British Journal of Psychology*, the drawings have been specially prepared for this volume, with his usual care, by Mr Edwin Wilson. I am indebted to the courtesy of Professor Ewald Hering and his publisher, Herr Wilhelm Engelmann, of Leipzig, for permission to reproduce the instructive coloured diagrams which appear as Plate I in his *Grundzüge der Lehre vom Lichtsinn*, now in course of publication ; and I should like to record my appreciation of the pains taken by the University Press to reproduce the various tints so successfully.

CHAPTER I

COLOUR VISION

THE sensations which we obtain from waves of light are divisible into two main classes or series, (*a*) colourless sensations and (*b*) colour sensations. At one end of the colourless series stands black, at the other end white, and between are ranged the various shades of grey. The series of colourless sensations may therefore be represented diagrammatically as a straight line, having black and white at the two extremes. The series of colour sensations, on the other hand, can only be represented in the form of a circle or oval. Starting, say, from a red stimulus R, we may introduce relatively more and more yellow Y and thus obtain a reddish-orange RO, an orange O, or a yellowish-orange OY sensation, or we may introduce relatively more and more blue B into the red and thus obtain a carmine C, a purple P or a violet V sensation. Thus from a red sensation we may pass towards pure blue or towards pure yellow, by continuous imperceptible changes. And from pure blue or pure yellow we may also pass by like changes towards pure green. The circle of changes in hue is hence complete. These changes are well indicated in Plates I and II. Pure red, pure yellow, pure green and pure blue are shown on the colour circle at the points marked r, y, g, b. The intermediate points in Plate I show different proportions of the two colours (e.g. $b : r = 1 : 3$), and the result of such admixture is shown at corresponding points in Plate II.

This series of colour sensations, shown also in fig. 1, follows the same order as those obtained by the decomposition of white light (as seen, for example, in the spectroscope or in the rainbow), with this important difference that in the spectrum the arrangement is not circular. The spectrum begins with red and ends with violet, and there are no spectral colours bridging these two extremes. As is well known, the stimulus at the red end of the spectrum consists of the longest waves of light, while at the violet end the light waves are shortest, the intervening colours being due to waves of intermediate length. Thus we may obtain an orange sensation by presenting to the eye the waves of spectral red and spectral yellow light simultaneously, or we may obtain precisely the same sensation by presenting to the eye the homogeneous waves of spectral orange light. (If the ear behaved analogously to the eye,

PLATE I

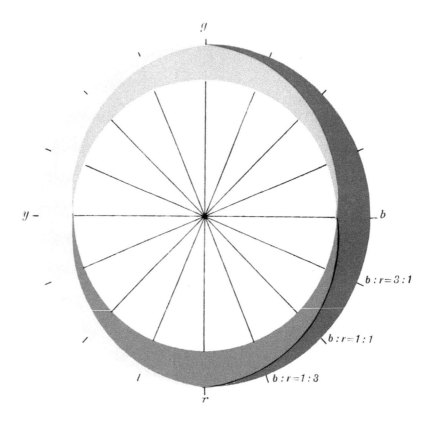

PLATE II

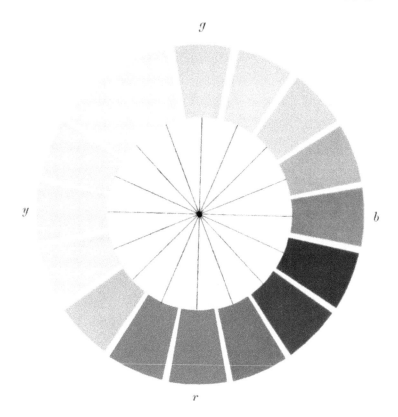

we should hear the tone d, alike when the note d was sounded and when the notes c and e were sounded simultaneously; but the ear of course behaves differently.) Similarly, we may obtain a greenish-blue sensation by employing as stimuli either a mixture of spectral blue and spectral green waves or the homogeneous spectral blue-green waves.

When, on the other hand, we combine any colour stimulus with another which lies more remote from it on our colour circle, we obtain a sensation gradually diminishing in hue and increasing in greyness; that is to say, there is less and less 'colour' in the resulting sensation, until ultimately a colour stimulus lying so far distant is reached that, when presented simultaneously with the other, it yields a perfectly colourless sensation of the black-white series. Every colour sensation may be said to have its antagonistic colour sensation, in the sense that when the corresponding stimuli simultaneously excite the same retinal area they produce merely a colourless sensation. The red of the extreme end of the spectrum and a certain bluish-green are antagonistic colours; so are purple and yellowish-green, violet and yellow, etc. These pairs of colours are also called 'complementary,' inasmuch as if one regards a sharply defined patch of one of these colours, and then turns the eye on to a colourless surface, the other member of the pair appears as a 'negative after-image.'

These observations suffice to indicate how colour sensations may vary not only in colour (or hue) but also in 'tint.' One colour sensation may be rich in colour, while another, although of the same colour, may be poor in it. This poverty is due to the simultaneous presence of some member of the colourless series. A red sensation will change in tint owing to the simultaneous presence of a grey. If the grey be light or white, the tint will be rose or pink; if it be dark or black, the tint will be brown. So too a blue, when fully saturated, yields a pure blue sensation; when mixed with the white, greys or black of the colourless series, it changes the sensation to a pale blue, or sky blue or a bluish-black tint. A 'highly saturated' colour is one which is rich in colour and contains a minimum of white.

But even when colour stimuli are pure, that is to say, even when the stimuli consist only of light waves of a uniform length and are freed by suitable filtering media from other waves and from white light, the colour sensations thus obtained differ from one another in yet another direction, namely in 'brightness.' It is obvious that the purest yellow sensation is brighter than the purest red or any other saturated colour sensation, and similarly that spectral green gives a brighter sensation than spectral blue. The totally colour-blind person sees the spectrum merely as shades of grey, which may be said to differ only in brightness. Indeed brightness is the one and only character in which sensations of the black-white series differ from one another.

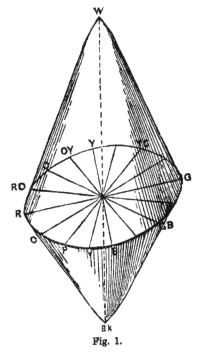

Fig. 1.

So far, then, we have reached the following conclusions. The series of colourless sensations varies

only in brightness; the coloured series varies both in
hue (colour) and in brightness; and by combining
stimuli which would separately yield colourless and
coloured sensations respectively, colour sensations
may be made to vary in tint. We may express these
conclusions geometrically in the form of a double
cone (fig. 1), the base of which R, RO, O, OY, Y,
etc., represents the circle of the colour sensations,
while the long axis joining the two apices W, Bk,
represents the linear series of colourless sensations.
The base is purposely tilted so that the extreme blue
end of the spectrum lies appreciably nearer than
the much brighter yellow to the black end of the
colourless series. Each spectral colour sensation
may thus be compared in brightness with a colourless
sensation,—a comparison which is actually realisable
in the laboratory. We can estimate the black-white
value even of the purest colour by direct comparison
and by other methods; that is to say, we can find
a grey which is of equal brightness to the colour in
question, and this grey, in turn, can be analysed into
simultaneously presented components of standard
white and black in definite proportions.

Under ordinary conditions, as we have seen,
yellow is the brightest colour sensation given by
any simple colour stimulus. But when the eye is
adapted to twilight, the point of maximal brightness
changes from yellow to green. At the same time,

blue colours appear lighter and red colours darker than when they are seen under ordinary illumination. Indeed so dark does the red end of the spectrum become that its extremity is invisible ; the red end of the spectrum thus appears shortened. These changes in the relative brightness of colours are known as the 'Purkinje phenomenon,' after the name of their discoverer[1]. They are not due merely to a reduction in the illumination of the colours. For by fixing transparent coloured patches in a partition-wall and viewing them by light transmitted from a neighbouring room, it is quite possible to reduce *their* illumination without altering the *general* illumination to which the eyes are exposed. Under these conditions the Purkinje phenomenon does not occur. It requires for its manifestation the adaptation of the eye to twilight. 'Dark-adaptation,' as it is called, is the essential factor for the production of the Purkinje phenomenon. Ultimately, if the illumination of the colours be sufficiently reduced and the eye be sufficiently dark-adapted, colours appear merely as shades of grey, those at the extreme red end of the spectrum being invisible, and the brightest grey appearing, as we have said, not in the yellow but in the region of the green. The process of

---

[1] The phenomenon can be readily observed at dusk on a summer's evening in a garden of variously coloured flowers.

dark-adaptation of the eye is a very slow one. Its independence of the size of the pupil can be easily demonstrated by dropping into the eye atropin which dilates the pupil through paralysis of the muscles governing it, or by placing before the eye an opaque disc pierced at its centre by a very small hole so as to form a minute artificial pupil of constant size. Dark-adaptation, and its converse process, light-adaptation, essentially depend on changes in the retinal apparatus. Light-adaptation takes place with great rapidity, while dark-adaptation has been said to be still incomplete even after an hour's stay in a perfectly dark room.

But not the whole of the retinal surface of our eye is susceptible to dark-adaptation. There is one small area, known as the 'fovea,' in which dark-adaptation is impossible. If a number of patches, coloured or colourless, be viewed in a nearly dark room by the sufficiently dark-adapted eye, it will be found that the particular patch to which the eye is turned is invisible, while the others are visible. As soon as the eye is turned to regard any one patch, that patch immediately vanishes. Now the fovea is the region of the retina which ordinarily receives light from a (not too large) object when the eye is turned to fixate it. Various other pieces of experimental evidence confirm the conclusion that, at the fovea, dark-adaptation, the Purkinje phenomenon and even vision under conditions of low illumination, are absent.

Now the structure of the fovea differs in one important respect from that of the rest of the retina. The sensory layer of the fovea consists solely of cells which from their shape are called cones ; the rest of the retina contains both cones and rods. We hence conclude that the rods constitute an apparatus for twilight vision. We find also that the rods are distinguished from the cones by the possession of a substance known as 'visual purple,' that this visual purple is rapidly bleached by daylight, that in darkness this colour becomes slowly restored, and that while red light has no effect, green light has the most powerful effect, on the bleaching of visual purple. Thus there is ample evidence to connect dark-adaptation and the consequent Purkinje phenomenon with the action of light on the visual purple of the retinal rods.

Further confirmation of this differentiation in function of the retinal rods and cones is obtained from a certain form of total colour-blindness, in which the eye is permanently dark-adapted, showing intolerance of bright light, a functionless or blind spot at the fovea, and (consequent on the absence of a definite fixation region for receiving the images of objects) a constant tremor of the eye-ball. In this form of colour-blindness, all colours appear as shades

of grey ; the brightest sensation is not, as in the
ordinary eye, obtained from the yellow, but as in
the dark-adapted eye from the green ; and the
extreme red end of the spectrum is invisible.   Thus
we have here a pathological condition in which the
cones are functionless and vision depends solely on
the activity of the rods.   This fact strongly supports
our conclusion that the rods are the end organs for
developing colourless sensations in the case of objects
seen under low illumination with the dark-adapted
eye, while the cones are responsible for colourless
and colour sensations under ordinary conditions of
daylight.

We can now proceed a step further in our analysis
of visual sensations, taking up more specifically the
problem of colour sensibility.   We have seen that the
pure sensations of colour derived from homogeneous
stimuli, unmixed with stimuli of the colourless series
of sensations, can be arranged in a circle (Plate II).
This circle contains at least a hundred and fifty
distinguishable hues.   The question arises whether
we have evidence that this enormous number of hues
is due to the combination in different ways and
degrees of a smaller number of 'primary' or
'fundamental' sensations, and if so, what these fundamental colour sensations are.   We turn, naturally
and perhaps justifiably, to abnormal conditions of
colour vision, to elicit an answer to these questions.

Besides the rare condition of total colour-blindness, two main varieties of congenital partial colour-blindness are known to occur. One is fairly common in males, occurring in about 4 per cent. of our European male population, and consists in blindness to red and green colours. The other is so exceedingly rare that we know little about it. Its characteristic is apparently a blindness to blue and yellow colours.

The red-green blind see a pure red or a pure green as grey. There is thus a region in the spectral green which they match with grey. The red which they match with grey is rather bluer than the red at the end of the spectrum ; it is the colour which is exactly complementary or antagonistic to the green just mentioned ; that is to say, it is that red which, when presented to the normal eye simultaneously with the just-mentioned green, gives rise to a colourless sensation. So far, then, we feel justified in assuming that a particular green and a particular red sensation are primary or fundamental. At first sight it may seem strange that the stimulus corresponding to the fundamental red sensation is not to be found in the spectrum, but to this fact we must not attach much importance. Our colour sensations have certainly developed regardless of the spectrum. We have seen what a number of colours occur in nature between the red and the blue, and it is for the purpose of securing adjustment to the outer

world, not to those abstract conditions hardly
realisable save within the laboratory, that our colour
sensibility has been evolved. That the extreme red
of the spectrum is too yellow to satisfy our notion
of a pure red is an easy matter of observation ; to
produce what is judged to be a pure red, some blue
must be mixed with spectral red.

So far all is plain sailing, but now we approach
the region of controversy. One theory of colour-
vision supposes that this particular red and its
antagonistic green, together with an apparently pure
yellow and its antagonistic blue, form the four
fundamental colour sensations. These four colours
are represented in Plate I, and from their combinations
in different proportions, the colours figured in Plate II,
and indeed the whole gamut of intermediate hues,
are procurable.

In favour of this theory its supporters claim for
consideration the colour sensibility of the normal
retina which lies outside the fovea, the 'peripheral'
retina. The extreme periphery of the retina is
totally colour-blind. If we fix a point with the
eye, and while we are steadily fixing it, introduce a
coloured patch so that the colour stimulus falls on
the outermost region of the retina, the patch is seen
as a grey. Now within this totally colour-blind zone
lies a zone which is red-green blind. If the coloured
patch be orange, it appears grey (as we have said)

when the stimulus falls on the extreme periphery of
the retina, but when introduced into less peripheral
areas it appears yellow; in this zone a yellowish-green
patch appears yellow, and a bluish-green, purple
or carmine patch appears blue. Finally, at the
centre, we reach a zone which is sensitive to the red
and green (if they occur) in the colour stimulus. Thus
we have three zones in the retina, an outer totally
colour-blind, an intermediate red-green blind zone
and a central zone of complete colour vision. Under
proper conditions, the zones for red and green are
found to be identical, and so are those for yellow and
blue[1].

Now it is easy to determine the exact hue of that
red and that green which appear colourless until
they reach the central zone, and to determine the
exact hue of that yellow and that blue which attain
their proper colour in the intermediate zone and do
not change when the stimulus is moved so as to fall
on to the central zone. The particular red and
green are found to be just those to which we have
already referred in considering the phenomena of
red-green blindness ; and the particular yellow and
blue are those two colours in which introspection on
the part of the normal individual fails to find a trace

---

[1] These zones are more accurately described as zones of colour
weakness. There is likewise recent evidence that red-green blind
individuals are rather colour-*weak* than colour-blind.

of red or green. There are thus two pairs of fundamental colour sensations, the antagonistic pair, red-green, and the antagonistic pair, yellow-blue. To this the theory adds a third pair, white-black. The theory supposes that while the stimuli for the fundamental red or fundamental green sensation act on the red-green apparatus, and the stimuli for the fundamental yellow or fundamental blue sensation act on the yellow-blue apparatus, they all act on the white-black apparatus. It supposes that the red-green, the yellow-blue and the white-black apparatus can each undergo changes in two directions. In the one direction the changes yield red, yellow and white sensations respectively, while changes in the reverse direction produce the sensations of green, blue and black respectively. Most colour stimuli of course act on all three apparatus, spectral red for instance, acting chiefly on the red-green so as to produce red, slightly on the yellow-blue so as to produce yellow and to some extent on the white-black so as to produce a grey. Thus we obtain the slightly yellowish red sensation afforded by spectral red. A blue-green stimulus, of course, can be found so that it excites the red-green and yellow-blue apparatus to an equal amount in a direction opposite to this action of spectral red. When such blue-green and spectral red stimuli simultaneously excite the retina, the theory accounts for the colourless sensation obtained,

for both the red-green and yellow-blue apparatus are
in equilibrium, since each is being equally urged in
opposite directions, and the stimuli act solely on the
white-black apparatus, causing the appearance of a
grey sensation.

Against this four-colour theory of Hering must
be set its three-colour rival, which owes its origin to
Young and its development principally to Helmholtz.
It is a well-known fact that, given a certain red, a
certain green, and a certain blue, we can by combining
them in different proportions obtain a white or any
hue we please. This physical fact has been believed
by many to be the basis of our colour sensations. A
certain red and blue, closely identical with those
chosen by the upholders of the four-colour theory, are
adopted as two of the fundamental colour sensations,
while the green, which is the third fundamental
sensation, lies on the yellow side of the green of the
four-colour theory.

Within the space at disposal, it is impossible to
enter into a detailed criticism of the merits and defects
of these rival theories. The three-colour theory in
a modified form accounts more satisfactorily for the
phenomena and varieties of partial colour-blindness.
On the other hand, the four-colour theory, in making
yellow and black fundamental sensations and in
accounting for the colour vision of the peripheral
retina, shows unquestionable superiority over its rival.

It errs, doubtless, in treating the colourless series as if they were on the same footing as the series of colour sensations, and in its explanation of the after-effects of sensations, but these difficulties are hardly overcome as yet in the three-colour theory. On the whole, it may be said that the evidence points to the existence of both a three- and a four-colour basis of colour vision. Some day, perhaps, we may be able to show how these two systems have been combined, one perhaps superadded at a later date in the course of evolution.

We turn now to an entirely different aspect of colour sensibility—its development in the individual and in the race. Over fifty years ago, the attention of students was directed to the very vague terminology of colour in the *Iliad*. Several words occur there for red, and one word, ξανθός, is definitely used for yellow; but a much less definite name, χλωρός, is used for green, and there is no definite word for blue or brown. These peculiarities of colour terminology have since been found not only to be characteristic of Homer but also to occur in ancient writings in very different parts of the world, for example in the Zendavesta and the Norse Edda. The conclusion has consequently been drawn that our colour sense has been evolved in comparatively modern times, that the sensations of red and yellow arose before the sensation of green, and that only at a much later date did the sensation of blue develop.

Although the colour sense of the ancient Greeks is beyond investigation, we can fortunately determine that of other primitive peoples of the present day, most of whom, it is interesting to note, show the same or similar defects in colour terminology as those deduced from the ancient writings of the civilised world. The Urális and Sholagas of Madras, for example, have a very definite word for red and a somewhat less definite word for yellow ; they have a word for green which may also be used for brown and grey and occasionally for black, but they have no word for brown, violet or light blue. The words they use for light blue are those they use also for green and black. So too among the Todas of Madras, definite words exist for red and yellow, many words are used to describe green, some of which are also applied to blue and to black, while violet and brown have no definite names.

The Murray Islanders of the Torres Straits have a definite word for red, two words for orange and yellow, a definite word for green, but no word of their own for blue. They use the same word to describe a jet-black and a bright blue colour. They have begun, however, to adopt the English word 'blue' which they reduplicate and pronounce as

'bŭlú-bŭlú.' Among the neighbouring islanders of
Kiwai, at the mouth of the Fly River, the colour
vocabulary is still more primitive. There are definite
words for red and for yellow, but the two words
commonly used to describe greens are also used for
white and black respectively and probably mean
merely 'light' and 'dark.' The word for black is
commonly used likewise for violet and blue, some
natives, however, using a word which they also apply
to green. Still more primitive appears the colour
vocabulary of an Australian tribe from the district of
Seven Rivers, on the Gulf of Carpentaria, who have
only three colour names ; the first being a definite
name for red, the second being applied to white,
yellow and green, and the third to black, blue and
violet. Thus the languages of Seven Rivers, Kiwai
and Murray Island show three distinct stages in the
evolution of colour names, and these stages correspond
in order to that of intellectual development among
the respective peoples. In the first language there is
but one definite colour name, namely, for red ; in the
second there are definite words for red and yellow ;
and in the third there are definite words for red,
yellow and green. But the native word for blue is
also used for black or green, or for both these colours,
and there are no definite words for brown or violet.

Of these various peoples, the Urális and Sholagas, the Todas and the Murray Islanders have been

investigated both for colour-blindness by means of wools, and for their sensitivity to faint colours by means of variously tinted slips of glass. The wool test is used in the following way. A certain skein of coloured wool is given to the subject, and he is asked to pick out from the rest of the coloured skeins those which appear to him of the same colour. Individuals who are red-green blind will match green with red, and, being insensitive to the red in carmine and orange and to the green in yellow-green, will match carmine with pale blue, orange with yellowish green, and so on. The experimenter is careful to observe not only the skeins which the subject finally selects, but also those which he takes up for the moment and then rejects. By this means suspicious cases may be detected which would otherwise escape notice. Of 150 male Murray Islanders tested, not a single case of red-green blindness was found ; of 81 male Urális and Sholagas only one was proved definitely to be red-green blind. Among male Europeans the frequency of red-green blindness is about four per cent. We see, then, that among the Murray Islanders and Urális and Sholagas red-green blindness is at all events much rarer than in Europe, if it be not completely absent in the former people. On the other hand, the Toda males, immediate neighbours of the Urális and Sholagas, show a remarkably high percentage (12·8 per cent.) of red-green blindness, 41 of 320 males examined being

defective. No clear case of yellow-blue blindness
was found, but there was a frequent tendency for the
natives to confuse reds with pinks, greens with blues,
blues with violets, and to match pale greens and
pale blues even with pinkish wools. The matches
may be partly due to a certain deficiency towards
blue; but they are also, in part at least, clearly the
outcome of defective nomenclature. It is a well-known
fact that colour-blind, e.g. red-green blind, people
become educated so as to recognise and to distinguish,
by differences in brightness and saturation, colours to
which they are insensitive. If asked to select reds, for
example, they may succeed quite well in picking out
a number of red wools. But if a skein is given them,
and no name is mentioned, they are much more likely
to reveal their defective sensibility. This difficulty is
of course only partly overcome when the subject,
instead of directly matching the standard skein with
the rest, himself gives the former a name and picks
out other wools to which he would give the same
name. As a matter of fact, such behaviour could be
seen to occur among the primitive peoples we are now
considering. And as they so commonly used the same
words for green and blue, the defects in colour vocabulary are at all events partly responsible for the
frequent tendencies towards colour confusion which
we have just mentioned.

The use of graded slips of glass, ranging from

white through the palest tints to obvious colours,
enables colour sensitivity to be readily and fairly
accurately determined. The subject looks with one
eye through a long narrow box divided by a longi-
tudinal partition, at the further end of which, on each
side of the partition, is an open orifice or window
illuminated by reflected white light. Into one of
these windows the experimenter introduces a colourless glass, into the other an obviously coloured glass,
say red. To the subject, of course, one window
appears white, the other red. The position of the
glasses is changed or maintained, without the knowledge of the subject, and five observations are taken.
If he correctly identifies the coloured window each
time, then a somewhat more palely tinted red glass is
used to replace the previous red glass. The coloured
glasses are standardised as being each equivalent to
so many units, two glasses say of ·20 unit giving the
same strength of colour as one glass of ·40 unit.
The colour is reduced after every five observations,
until the subject makes at least one mistake in five
answers. Then five more answers are obtained, and
if another mistake is made, this glass is taken as a
measure of the subject's sensitivity. Two wrong
answers in ten, therefore, determine the colour
threshold. By this, or by a closely similar, procedure
the following results have been obtained, the units of
colour in the coloured glass serving as a numerical
measure of this threshold :—

	41 English	14 Urális and Sholagas	47 Todas	18 Murray Islanders
Red	·27	·31	·32	·18
Yellow	·17	·26	·29	·26
Blue	·31	·66	·53	·60

Unfortunately no test has yet been made for green. But the results for the three colours which have been used show that the primitive peoples are very much less sensitive for blue and somewhat less sensitive for yellow than the English while their sensitiveness to red is about equal to or greater than that of the English. The most striking difference between the English and the primitive peoples is of course in the relative insensitiveness of the latter to blue.

Now there are several reasons which may be advanced to explain this apparent insensitiveness to blue. We may be inclined to connect it directly with the absence of a definite colour name for blue, and to ascribe both not so much to sensory deficiency as to lack of interest in this particular colour. The most attractive and conspicuous objects in nature are red and yellow. Green and blue are the colours of foliage, sky and sea; such widely extended surfaces behave as backgrounds of colour and tend to escape especial notice. Of all coloured objects, blood is perhaps the most striking and plays the most important part in the ceremonial of primitive people

Red and to a less extent yellow are the commonest pigments used for decorative purposes among uncivilised communities. For these reasons it is hardly surprising that red and yellow have been the first colours to receive specific names. Greens and blues are less useful, less attractive and less interesting. Wherefore, it may be argued, the natives come to neglect weak blues and greens and to observe the faintest trace of red.

But this explanation proves unsatisfactory. In the first place, primitive peoples are not merely deficient in sensitiveness to blue, but also slightly to yellow. (This however may be accounted for by the fact that the yellow glass used was of a distinctly greenish tint, and by the supposition that they are also relatively insensitive to green.) In the second place, even where a fairly definite word for blue occurs, as among the modern Egyptians, a still more marked insensitivity to blue, may be present, as the following figures attest:—

	41 English	26 Egyptians
Red	·27	·29
Yellow	·17	·26
Blue	·31	·85

Now the ancient Egyptians (and the modern also) appear to have evolved a definite word for blue. They frequently used blue pigment in their pottery, on their stone figures, and—eccentrically it is true—

in colouring the surface of their reliefs and their sculptures. (We have yet to discover the origin of the extraordinary schemes of colouration which were employed among ancient civilisations and resulted in blue bulls, green men and the like.) Consequently there seems no direct connexion between apparent insensitivity to blue and a want of interest in the colour. It is indeed sufficiently obvious that there are many sensations to which we are indifferent and to which we have never given special names, but which we can experience even when the stimuli which produce them are very weak. Names are only given when nomenclature serves some useful purpose. We, cattle-loving people, have for centuries past used various names to describe the colour of our horses, yet the majority of primitive peoples have no specific word for brown. That of course does not imply that they are insensitive to brown; indeed in all probability they are rather more sensitive to it than Europeans are.

It has been suggested that the deficient sensibility of coloured races to blue arises from the stronger pigmentation of the 'yellow spot' of the retina, in consequence of which blue and green rays of light are more strongly absorbed on reaching the retina in comparison with red and yellow, and thus a certain insensitivity to blue and green would arise. It seems quite likely that this explanation is correct. But we

cannot, if we adopt it, attempt to derive defects of
colour nomenclature from the same cause, inasmuch
as some European languages, as an example of which
we may cite modern Welsh, have no word for blue,
or, as in certain parts of Germany, confuse violet
and brown.

Finally we may turn to the colour sense of European
infants and children in the hope of further additions
to our knowledge.   Infants from 22 to 60 weeks old
have been tested by holding or placing before them
pairs of woollen balls or wooden bricks of different
colours, and by observing which colour is preferred.
Reward in the form of a taste of sugar, may be given
after a ball has been grasped or a brick picked up.
Prolonged experiments with coloured objects, and
with objects painted in various shades of the colourless (white-black) series, appear to show that at
a very early age,—probably long before the sixth
month,—infants grasp red and yellow objects in
preference to green and blue and colourless (even
bright white) objects, while blue is at this stage
hardly if at all preferred to white objects.   Probably
at this, and certainly at a somewhat later stage, the
infant's preferences are dictated not by brightness
but by colour.   For example a babe, of about the
55th week, was found to grasp a yellow brick far
more frequently than a white one, when both were
simultaneously exhibited, although the latter must

have appeared brighter to it than the former. On the other hand, a blue brick, although at first picked up more frequently than a white one, soon lost favour. Thus, prolonged experiment showed that blue was at first preferred solely on the score of novelty of colour, while yellow was chosen with increased instead of with diminished frequency at successive sittings. The same babe distinctly preferred a brighter to a darker colourless brick. Consequently the preferences for coloured objects, at all events at this age, are determined by colour, not merely by brightness.

Such experiments however afford little evidence of colour sensibility. Because a babe picks up blue and grey equally often, or because at an early stage it picks up reds and yellows in preference to greens and blues, we cannot infer that it is colour-blind, or less sensitive, to greens and blues. It may well be that reds and yellows are more interesting and attractive than greens and blues.

English children of five years of age and upwards have been investigated by the same test as has been applied to primitive people for determining the colour thresholds, but the results do not differ from those obtained from English adults as regards their relative sensitivity to red, yellow and blue. We find no trace of that remarkable deficiency in sensitivity to blue (and slight insensitivity to greenish yellow)

which we have found among the adults of coloured
peoples. English children have also been tested for
colour-blindness by matching wools, and have been
found to make the same confusions in respect to
bluish colours as occur (p. 20) among primitive
peoples.

We seem justified, then, in concluding that
deficient interest in blues and greens is mainly
responsible for the defects in colour vocabulary
and the colour matches characteristic of primitive
peoples. But we find reason to doubt whether the
defective sensibility to blues and greens which exists
in primitive peoples can also be attributed to lack of
interest in the stimuli concerned, and hence whether
with sufficient interest or experience the thresholds
would have changed their value. There is no doubt
that practice increases the facility of discriminating
faint shades of colour, just as it is the basis of the
education of the tea-taster or the wine-expert. It is
impossible to foretell the potentialities of the human
mind which are undeveloped owing to deficient
interest or practice. Under a British teacher, for
example, the Murray Island children proved themselves rather more expert at arithmetic than English
children of the same age, but the islanders had no
words in their own language save one and two to
express numbers. Is it possible then, that the low
threshold for blue is due merely to their accustomed

general inattention to this colour? The probability is that this explanation is inadequate, for we have just seen that English children are similarly un-attracted to blue, without, however, showing deficient sensitivity to the colour. We can but conclude that the special insensitivity to blue (and to green as shown in the greenish yellow test employed) is due to some special cause, perhaps to pigmentation of the sensory epithelium as has been already sug-gested.

Experiments which have been performed upon animals have hitherto thrown little light on the development of colour vision. One great difficulty lies in determining whether differences in their be-haviour are due to differences in colour or in bright-ness merely. It is only in recent work that adequate attention has been paid to this point. Another and insuperable difficulty is our powerlessness to deter-mine sensation qualities in animals other than our-selves. Even among men, there is reason to believe that no two subjects have *precisely* the same colour sense. A *fortiori* when dogs, mice, birds or crayfish are proved to be capable of distinguishing one colour from another, we are not in the least justified in con-cluding that these colours appear equally different to these various animals, or that their experiences of colour are comparable to our own.

Experiments on the colour vision of the higher animals have been performed by training the animal to react in a prescribed way, say to enter a compartment coloured in a given hue, perhaps rewarding or punishing it according as it enters the right or the wrong compartment. When once the animal has learnt to react to a given colour, the experimenter studies the degree of correctness with which it is able to react in the simultaneous presence of one or more colours or greys illuminating other compartments. In other experiments, especially on lower animals, the reaction is obtained by offering food on tiles or in forceps of a given colour, or by colouring the food. In the lowest organisms, experiment is confined merely to observation of their movements when the cage or trough is illuminated by lights of different colours.

In this place, it is impossible to set forth the various conclusions which have been reached by different workers. They agree in finding that in regard to colour sensibility animals differ widely among one another and from ourselves. The most recent experiments upon dogs appear to show that during the early days of training they react so exclusively to differences of brightness that at this stage of experiment they appear to be totally colour-blind. It is only later, after a period of prolonged training, that they show themselves capable of reacting to differences of colour. There is no evidence in all the work which has been devoted to animal colour vision that red and green vision is generally weak or sometimes absent. Yet one might have expected that red-green vision would prove to be the last in the course of evolution to be acquired, considering the relatively great frequency of red-green blindness in man. Thus neither in animals, nor among children or savages, is there evidence of a development of the colour sense along a definite path. There is no evidence that man has acquired his colour vision say by an early evolution of the red (or blue) sense, later by the appearance of the green, and lastly by the appearance of the blue (or red) sense. Perhaps the earliest condition was one of colourless vision, all objects appearing as shades of a homogeneous light. It was only later that the growing experience and needs of the race and of the individual enabled him to differentiate colours one from another, and to distinguish colour from colourlessness. We have seen that, though red and green vision is so unstable in man, yet red is the most attractive of all colours. No doubt, we have to distinguish between the primary physiological bases of colour vision, and the fullest possible manifestation of their respective functions. The former may be installed, long before

the individual or the race has reached the stage when
it is capable of appreciating *all* the various sensations
which such an apparatus permits him to differentiate.
That is to say, we have to distinguish the evolution
of the upper from the lower systems of that vast
unravelled complex—the cerebro-retinal apparatus—
which is responsible for our colour vision.

CHAPTER II

TOUCH, TEMPERATURE AND PAIN

By moving a cold blunt-pointed rod over the skin, it is easy to show that cutaneous sensibility to cold is far from uniform. The entire surface is sensitive to changes of temperature, but here and there we frequently meet with spots of exquisite sensitivity, giving us, so to speak, lightning flashes of cold. It is easy to mark the position of these 'cold spots' on the skin and thus to obtain a map of their distribution. Some cold spots are found to be very much more sensitive than others; and the position of these can be repeatedly confirmed at different sittings. But the less sensitive cold spots may escape the subject's notice on another occasion owing to unfavourable conditions, especially to general fatigue.

The existence of similar 'heat spots' may be demonstrated by exploration of the skin with a blunt-pointed instrument which is maintained at a temperature of about 45° C.[1] But whereas the cold spots are often closely grouped in chains and clusters, the heat spots are much less numerous. They are so isolated that their position is generally re-discoverable without difficulty. They are less variable than the cold spots in sensitivity.

There are also spots on the skin which are especially sensitive to light touches, and their distribution is found to be again different from that of the cold spots and from that of the heat spots. On hairy parts of the skin a 'touch spot' is to be found over the site of each hair root. The skin should be shaven before the examination for touch spots is begun, as otherwise the hairs may be accidentally touched and the touch spots be thus stimulated unwittingly. A few touch spots occur between hairs; they are also met with in abundance on certain hairless regions, e.g. on the palm and sole. Touch spots are best demonstrated by exploring the skin with a fine hair, mounted in a wooden handle. A series of such hairs may be prepared, varying in the pressure they are capable of exerting on the skin. This

---

[1] Centigrade degrees may be expressed in the Fahrenheit scale by multiplying them by nine-fifths and adding 32 to the product; thus 45° C. = 111° F. The following equations may also be useful in later chapters for readers who are not familiar with the metric system: 1 millimetre = 0·0394 inch; 1 centimetre = 0·394 inch; 1 metre = 39·4 inches; 1000 cubic centimetres = 1·76 pint; 1 gram = 15·43 grains.

pressure can be calculated by pressing the hair on one scale of a balance while a variable weight occupies the other scale. Knowing the cross section of the hair, it is easy to calculate the tension or the pressure per unit area (grams per square millimetre) which the hair exerts on the skin.

Lastly, a system of spots, far more numerous and more variable in sensitivity than the cold, heat, or touch spots, can with some uncertainty be demonstrated on the skin. These we may term 'pain spots.' Their sensitivity may be measured by hair stimuli, hairs of course being chosen for the purpose which exert considerably greater pressure than those used for demonstrating touch spots. But the pain spots are so numerous, and so variable in sensitivity, that any given map can only be said to represent the distribution of those which respond to the strength of the particular exploring stimulus. It is possible that every point of the skin would produce a pain sensation if the stimulus were sufficiently intense.

Two other important investigations in cutaneous sensibility must be briefly alluded to. In order to determine the accuracy of localisation, the subject keeps his eyes closed throughout the experiment and attempts to point to a spot at which the experimenter has just touched him ; or opening his eyes, the subject endeavours to mark this spot on a life-size photograph of the region (e.g. the arm) under examination.

After a series of touches it is easy to determine the direction and amount of the subject's error.

We have also to determine the least distance at which two blunted compass points applied to the skin can be appreciated as two. If the points are too close, the skin appears to be touched at only one spot. The least distance at which a double touch can be felt as such gives what is called the 'spatial threshold.' A satisfactory method of determining this threshold is described on page 99.

If a nerve supplying a given sensory surface of the skin be cut across, that surface is immediately robbed of all sensations of touch, cold, heat and pain. The surface can then be stimulated with a hair or with a hot or cold point without the stimulus evoking the slightest sensation. Freezing of the part only produces a vague aching. A fold of the subject's skin may be gently raised between finger and thumb and even powerfully squeezed; yet the subject experiences no sensation of touch or pain. If, however, the touch, e.g. of a finger or a pencil, be so applied that pressure is communicated to the tissues underlying the skin, a sensation is at once evoked; and this sensation is not appreciably different from the results of similar pressure over a normal area of skin.

Thus there is a 'deep' sensibility in addition to and, so far as nerve supply goes, different from the 'superficial,' truly cutaneous, sensibility which we have hitherto been studying. This deep sensibility consists in sensitiveness to pressure and, when this pressure exceeds a certain limit, in sensitiveness to pain. If only the touch be heavy enough to produce a sensation, it can be localised with remarkable accuracy. The subject can also satisfactorily discriminate between the positions of two pressures applied successively to neighbouring spots of the skin. Yet, despite the unchanged power of localisation and the unchanged spatial threshold for successive pressures, the subject is incapable of distinguishing double pressures when they are made simultaneously, and he is incapable of determining the relative size of different objects successively placed on the skin of the affected area.

Let us now study the return of sensitivity in a definite skin-area of a human arm which, for purposes of scientific study, had expressly been made insensitive by surgical section of a nerve supplying it. The salient features that marked the process of recovery may be summarised as follows :

Forty-three days after the operation the loss of cutaneous pain began to diminish in extent, the boundaries of the painless area retreating, and islets of sensibility to pain making their appearance within the insensitive area.

One hundred and twelve days after the operation, there was still further improvement in sensibility to pricks, and also evidence of the first return of sensibility to cold.

One hundred and thirty-seven days after the operation, the whole area had recovered sensibility to cold, but was insensitive to heat. Only a very small area now remained which was insensitive to pricks.

One hundred and sixty-one days after the operation, a patch of the affected area first became sensitive to very light touch. Heat spots also began to appear.

One hundred and ninety days after the operation, cold was everywhere appreciable, and thenceforth the number of heat and cold spots increased rapidly.

At this point, therefore, we have reached a stage when the touch spots were just beginning to resume their function, and the sensations of cold, heat and pain spots were already fairly restored. Let us pause at this stage to describe in greater detail the condition of this subject's cutaneous sensibility.

We will begin with pain. A stimulus more intense than usual was found needful to elicit pain; that is to say, sensibility to pain over the affected area was subnormal. But when the pain sensation did occur, it was found to be abnormally unpleasant and diffuse, and to be referred to distant parts. Indeed its unpleasantness was often extreme. A prick applied to the forearm was not felt as a prick at all; it produced only a widely radiating pain over the thumb.

Coming now to the temperature sensations, we have seen that sensibility to heat returned somewhat later than that to cold. It was evident that at the stage which we are now considering, sensibility depended entirely on the reactions of heat and cold spots. The heat spots were most readily stimulated by temperatures ranging between 44° C. and 48° C. Only under the most favourable conditions did a stimulus of 37° C. act on a heat spot. No cold spot ever reacted to temperatures of or above 27° C. Indeed when sensibility to cold first reappeared, no sensations of cold could be produced by temperatures above 20° C. The sensations of heat and cold thus produced were characterised by diffuseness and by reference to remote parts.

Over the normal body surface, the temperature stimulus which we call neutral (neither hot nor cold) varies within wide limits according to the state of adaptation of that surface[1]. If we immerse one hand in warm water, the other in cool, and after a few minutes plunge both into a single vessel of water of some intermediate temperature, this water feels cool to the former hand, and warm to the latter. But such adaptation was proved impossible at the present stage of recovery in the affected area. The heat spots

[1] E.g. the neutral temperature within the mouth is normally 86°·9 C. (98°·4 F.); that on different parts of the skin surface varies between 27° C. and 32° C.

never reacted to temperatures below 37° C. when the area had been exposed to cold ; the cold spots never reacted to temperatures above 27° C. when the area had been exposed to heat.

As regards light touch, we have seen that, up to the 161st day after the operation, the affected area was completely insensitive. On this day dragging cotton wool across the arm first produced a curious tingling sensation, which was referred to remote parts. This sensation could not be evoked after the affected area had been shaved. It was proved absent in a portion of the area which happened to be hairless, and was therefore due solely to stimulation of the hairs.

Thus at this stage of recovery of cutaneous sensibility, the affected area was sensitive to pain, heat, cold and to the light touch of hairs. It was insensitive to moderately warm or cool stimuli, and it had lost the normal power of adaptability to temperature. Only the extremes of temperature proved adequate stimuli. Where the spots were absent, no temperature sensation was obtainable. The area was insensitive to touch over hairless or shaven regions.

We have seen that so long as the area was sensitive only to deep pressure, localisation was accurate. But with the return of sensibility to heat, cold, superficial pain and the touch of hairs, it became quite abnormal. The sensations were now of a diffuse character, radiating widely and referred to a distant area.

The recognition of the relative size of objects was lost, and so too was the ability to discriminate between the two points of the compass. Touch with a single point was repeatedly declared to be a double touch. Moreover, double touches were declared to be single ones, even at distances at which double touches could be accurately appreciated before when deep sensibility alone remained.

We have, then, first a stage of 'deep' sensibility when only deep pressure and deep pain can be experienced, localised and discriminated; and later a stage of what has been called 'protopathic' sensibility which is characterised by a diffuse and distantly localised response to the touch of hairs, to the extremes of temperature and to superficial painful stimuli, but which is irresponsive to light touches over hairless regions and to moderate temperatures, and is incapable of adaptation to temperature, of accurate localisation and of spatial discrimination.

We turn now to a small triangular region of the affected area which proved to be in a condition of peculiar interest and importance. The one feature which this region shared with the rest of the affected area was its sensitiveness to deep pressure and pain; in other respects it proved entirely different. It was completely insensitive to cutaneous painful (e.g.

electrical) stimuli. A prick caused no pain, but
merely gave rise to the recognition of a point.
Extremes of heat and cold could not be felt. To all
temperatures below 22° C. it remained insensitive.
If the temperature exceeded 49° C. it was declared
to be merely a touch, or sometimes to be slightly
warm but rapidly becoming neutral—neither warm
nor cool; whereas a temperature of 36° C. (below
the minimal stimulus for a heat spot) was felt as
warm. Not until 173 days after the operation did
sensibility to temperatures below 22° C. reappear, and
for the first time was a cold spot now discovered, in
this area. Twenty-five days later the first heat spot
reappeared, and thenceforth the region quickly
returned to its normal sensibility. From the first,
this region was distinguished from the rest of the
affected area by its sensitiveness to cutaneous tactile
stimuli. Cotton wool and hair stimuli produced
sensations which, in the power of localisation and
spatial discrimination, and in the absence of remote
reference and radiation, were identical with the
sensations evoked from a normal skin area. The
only difference consisted in a slight diminution in
tactile sensibility and spatial discrimination.

Thus this triangle presented the very characteristics which were found lacking in the protopathic
sensibility of the rest of the affected area : it showed
sensibility to superficial touch, to warmth and

probably, under favourable conditions of adaptation, to coolness, accurate power of localization and spatial discrimination. This form of sensibility has been termed 'epicritic' sensibility, because its special feature consists in the power of correct localization and discrimination of cutaneous stimuli. This small region in the affected area, at a certain stage of recovery, was found to possess the epicritic system and to lack the protopathic, while the rest, the greater part of the area, possessed the protopathic but lacked the epicritic system of cutaneous sensibility. The small region to which we have just alluded was only discovered under the favourable conditions of experimental nerve division and protracted expert examination. There is evidence, however, of the existence of such areas in other cases of nerve division, and in certain regions of the normal body.

We have traced the return of protopathic sensibility over the greater part of the affected area. Obviously this system regenerates with greater speed than that of epicritic sensibility. Over a small triangular region only, protopathic sensibility had disappeared, leaving, as we have seen, the epicritic sensibility in an isolated condition for examination. Exactly one year after the operation, epicritic sensibility began to return in the rest of the affected area. A patch on the forearm proved sensitive to cotton wool after being shaven, the previous tingling and tendency to remote reference having now disappeared. But with the onset of winter eight months later, the area in great part returned temporarily to its previous condition of sensibility. 407 days after the operation, sensibility to temperatures of and somewhat below 37° C. began to develop, with accurate localisation and absence of the former radiation and reference to remote regions. But again, with the onset of winter, the arm tended to revert to its former condition. During this season, only on bright and warm days could the sensibility to temperatures between 33° C. and 37° C. be demonstrated. Experimentally too it could be shown that cold threw the recovering area into its earlier protopathic state, but in course of time the epicritic system proved increasingly stable.

We see, then, that in the sensibility of the normal skin two distinct systems are involved, either of which may appear alone, divorced from the other. The suggestion may be entertained that these two systems have been acquired at different times in the evolution of cutaneous sensibility. It may well be that epicritic sensibility is the more recent, as it is the more easily lost and the last to be regained, being absent in certain 'primitive' situations, e.g. over the inner surface of the viscera where only extremes of heat and cold can be experienced, where pain is felt provided the stimulus be appropriate, and diffuse radiation and remote reference are characteristic features of sensibility. The addition of epicritic sensibility breaks down this nexus of stimulated areas with remote parts. Accurate localisation becomes possible, and vagueness and complexity in psychic experience give way before definiteness and simplicity.

This conception, if true, adds one more link to the chain of evidence in favour of the view that what we are disposed from its simplicity to regard as elementary is actually often the later and more advanced. Undifferentiated confusion is the keynote of early life, to be dispelled with the development of the species and the individual.

CHAPTER III

THE MÜLLER-LYER ILLUSION

If two horizontal lines, WX, YZ (fig. 2), of equal length be compared, no obvious difference in length is apparent. But if 'arrow heads' or 'feather heads' be affixed to the ends of either of these lines, as at AB, CD, then a very striking difference in length at once arises. AB appears distinctly shorter, CD distinctly longer than the plain horizontal line, and *a fortiori* AB appears very much shorter than CD. This apparent difference in length between AB and CD constitutes the Müller-Lyer illusion, so called after the name of an early investigator of its nature. Modifications of the illusion are also shown in the same figure.

Of the various methods adopted by psychologists to measure the Müller-Lyer illusion, probably the following is the most reliable. One of the lines, e.g. AB, has a constant length, say of 50 millimetres[1]. The length of the other line CD can be varied at will by

---

[1] See footnote to p. 38 for corresponding British measure.

the experimenter, before it is exhibited to the subject. Let us suppose that five different lengths of *CD* are chosen, measuring 40, 41, 42, 43, and 44 mm. respectively. Each of these five lengths is presented ten times in irregular order to the subject, each time with the constant length *A B*, and fifty answers are obtained from the subject by the experimenter. The subject

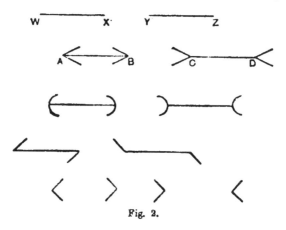

Fig. 2.

may answer that one of the two lines is 'distinctly longer,' 'longer,' 'slightly longer,' 'slightly shorter,' 'shorter,' or 'distinctly shorter' than the other, or that there is 'no difference' between them. Thus the experimenter records the answers of the subject in terms of one of the two lines exhibited.

Under such conditions, however, instead of comparing the constant line AB with the variable line
CD, the subject tends to pay exclusive attention to
the latter. It is found that he judges of the relative
lengths by forming an absolute judgment of CD, or
by comparing the CD exhibited at the moment with
other lengths of CD previously exhibited. It is
therefore desirable to intersperse irregularly in the
above series a second series of observations which
differs only from the former in that CD is now constant
and AB becomes the variable ; CD measuring say 40
mm. and the lengths of the five variables being, let
us say, 46, 47, 48, 49, and 50 mm., but differing, of
course, according to the size of the illusion in the
subject under investigation.

Thus in a complete series, constituting a single
day's experiment, one hundred answers are obtained.
The following is an example of such a series, the
lengths of the constant and variable lines being those
which we have given above. The letters S, L, denote
that the variable appears 'distinctly shorter,' 'distinctly longer' ; s, l, indicate answers 'shorter,'
'longer' ; (s), (l), mean 'slightly shorter,' 'slightly
longer' ; n means 'no difference.' The answers are
sorted out subsequently and may be thus tabulated.

AB as constant (50 *mm.*).

Lengths of
CD in mm.

40.	S	s	s	S	(s)	s	(s)	(s)	s	s
41.	(s)	s	s	s	n	(l)	(s)	(s)	s	(s)
42.	s	(s)	(l)	n	(l)	(l)	(l)	l	(s)	l
43.	l	L	(l)	(l)	L	n	l	(l)	n	l
44.	l	l	L	(l)	L	L	(l)	(l)	l	l

CD as constant (40 *mm.*).

Lengths of
AB in mm.

46.	s	s	S	s	s	(s)	s	S	s	S
47.	s	(s)	(s)	S	n	(s)	n	(s)	s	s
48.	(l)	s	l	(l)	(s)	(s)	n	(s)	n	(s)
49.	l	(l)	l	l	(s)	l	L	l	l	(l)
50.	l	L	L	(l)	l	l	L	l	(l)	L

The above figures were actually obtained during a single day's experiment[1]. From them it is easy to determine the length of the variable line which appears equal to the constant, and thus by subtraction of the constant from the variable to measure the illusion.

Now it has been asserted that the Müller-Lyer illusion is due to the influence of the arms (the arrow heads or feather heads) on the movements of the

---

[1] It is very surprising what a difference an increase in the length of the variable line by one millimetre produces in the proportion of the various kinds of answers; this feature, we may here observe, is still more striking when the lines are only exhibited momentarily to the subject.

eyes while they are traversing the figures.   In the case of the arrow head figure AB, the movements of the eyes are said to be hampered or restricted, while in the case of the feather head figure CD, they have been considered to be freer and to be encouraged to move beyond the ends of the horizontal line.   Consequently the sensations of eye movement are different in the two cases, and the horizontal line in AB appears shorter than that in CD.

Were this the case the illusion should be much greater when the subject has the opportunity of moving his eyes across the figures than when the figures are exhibited for a very brief time, e.g. flashed momentarily on to a screen, so that all possibility of eye movement is prevented.   But experiment has demonstrated beyond question that the illusion in momentary exposure of the figures is invariably much greater than that occurring in prolonged exposure.

Further, after the subject has overcome the obvious initial difficulties of fixating the eyes preparatory to receiving the figures in momentary exposure, the method of momentary exposure always gives more reliable and more decisive results than can be obtained by the method of prolonged exposure. The subject feels that it is possible to answer without hesitation, to decide almost intuitively during momentary exposure; whereas with the same figures during

M   4 prolonged exposure he vacillates and cannot easily reach a definite opinion. Corresponding to this introspection, the experimenter finds that the hundred answers returned by the subject during any one day's series of experiments are much more consistent with each other in momentary than in prolonged exposures, and that in the former there is a smaller number of 'slightly longer (or shorter),' answers and a greater number of 'distinctly longer (or shorter)' answers than in the latter.

In the face of these results, it is impossible to accept the explanation which attributes the illusion to differences in freedom or restriction of eye movement. Moreover, this explanation receives little or no support from experiments in which the eyes of a subject were kinematographically photographed so that it was possible by means of photographs to study his eye movements, while he moved his eyes to and fro, from end to end, of ABC (fig. 3); he being enjoined to pay special attention to the fixation of the points A, B, and C. It is true that the movements were found to be somewhat freer and less interrupted along the feather head portion than along the arrow head portion of the figure, and that they tended to be prematurely arrested and diverted from the horizontal by the arrow heads. But there were often subsequent additional movements of the eyes, which, when taken into account, made it difficult to attribute the illusion to sensations of eye movement. Moreover, the eye movements were found to be far too inconstant in character to be the cause of the illusion.

Similar experiments yielding still more decisive results in this connexion have been conducted, in which the eyes of a subject were kinematographically photographed while they were carrying out to and fro movements between a point A and another B (fig. 4), fixating B for a moment then returning to

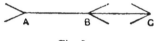

Fig. 3.

fixate A, and so on. It is unlikely that our sensations of eye movement are so delicate as they must needs be if our estimations of spatial magnitude are dependent on them[1]. In these experiments it was found that the eyes were very far from being still during an attempt to fixate a point, that the character of the eye movements during intended fixation was incon-

[1] Fine black parallel lines, separated from each other by distances equal to their own diameter, can be distinguished when the angle through which the eye would have to be turned (if spatial discrimination depended on sensibility to eye movement), so that the images of two neighbouring lines might successively fall on the same retinal spot, amounts to about one minute. At the shoulder (perhaps the most sensitive of our joints to movement) an angular movement of about twenty minutes is the smallest perceivable.

stant, and that the two eyes did not fixate a point in exactly the same manner, nor did they pass from it at the same moment or travel from it to the other point at exactly the same speed.

When lines were added to the points as at D or F (fig. 4) the fixation of these points became more unsteady ; but, unfortunately for the eye movement hypothesis (for the figures CD, EF, contain the essential features of the Müller-Lyer illusion), it was

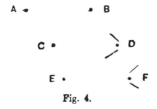

Fig. 4.

found that the eye movement did not differ obviously in character according to the inclination of the oblique lines.

There is much other evidence to show what little information is obtainable from movements of our eyes. For example, if an individual be introduced into a dark room and if he fixate a point of light which is then extinguished, a considerable amount of eye movement unconsciously occurs although he believes that he is still fixating the spot where the point of light was situated.

There is indeed reason for believing that eye
movements are rather the result than the cause of
our estimation of small spatial magnitudes, and that
the primary basis of such estimation is to be sought
in the sensibility of the cerebro-retinal apparatus and
not merely in that of the muscular apparatus of
the eye.   To what extent eye movements influence
spatial experience in very early life and what part
they play in the judgment of larger magnitudes are
questions at present unsettled and presenting considerable difficulty.

Additional light is thrown on the nature of the
Müller-Lyer illusion by studying the effects of practice.
If the series of hundred judgments to which we have
already alluded be repeated day after day, the illusion
will be found progressively to diminish and in the
end to disappear completely.   After about fourteen
days' practice, the line *A B* (fig. 2) appears equal to
the line *CD* when the lines are actually of equal
length.   At the end of such practice, the subject
finds it incredible that he should have given the
judgments which were obtained from him at the
outset of the experiments.

But this happens only under conditions of
prolonged exposure.   Practice in the momentary
exposures, lasting even for eighteen or twenty days,
does not produce any significant change in the
extent of the illusions.

These striking changes brought about by practice can occur without the subject being conscious of any alteration in his mode of procedure. The one important feature which introspection may reveal is that practice enables the subject to limit his attention to the horizontal line and to disregard the arms. Finally he may feel a complete mastery over the figure. And this piece of introspection probably supplies the key to the nature of the illusion. It suggests that, in our judgment of the length of a part of the figure, that judgment is unconsciously influenced by the size of the whole.

If this explanation be correct the illusion should diminish, the more prominently the horizontal line is drawn in relation to the arms. This is found to be the case ; and the illusion is markedly reduced if the horizontal line be presented in a colour different from that in which the arms are drawn. The illusion should also be greater during momentary exposure than during prolonged exposure which allows time for the independent apprehension of the several parts of the figure. This we have already stated (p. 49) to be the case.

We may apply the same explanation to the results obtained by determining the size of the illusion in civilised and savage communities. Among very primitive peoples, e.g. those of the Torres Straits, the illusion turns out to be distinctly smaller than in

England, while less primitive peoples, e.g. the Todas of Madras, stand midway, in size of the illusion, between the Torres Straits Islanders and Englishmen.

For the purpose of carrying out determinations in the field, an apparatus made of white xylonite has been used, in which a part slides like the lid of a box in and out of a shallow framework (fig. 5). The subject pushes the lid into its frame or draws the lid out of the frame (an equal number of observations, say five,

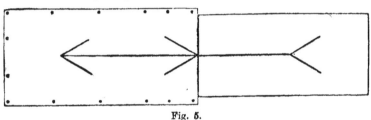

Fig. 5.

being made by each procedure) until the two parts of the Müller-Lyer figure appear equal. From a scale drawn on the back of the instrument, the experimenter can at once determine the extent of the illusion. The mean of the ten observations made by each subject is taken.

It is probably because of his unfamiliarity with geometrical figures that the savage experiences the Müller-Lyer illusion in a less degree than the civilised man ; for him such figures have less 'meaning.'

Consequently he is less influenced by the figure as a whole when estimating the length of one of its parts. He is able to attend more exclusively to the horizontal line and is less influenced by the presence of the arms. For him the task is of a more elementary character than for the civilised man.

There is another cause of the greater complexity of the task for the civilised man, and this leads to a different result. It consists in the fact that he is more apt to suspect or to be already acquainted with the illusion, and consequently, in some instances, to attempt by various means to overcome it. The result is that the extent of the illusion is found to vary much less among the individuals of a primitive than among those of a civilised community, and similarly to vary less among civilised children than among civilised men.

In the study of the Müller-Lyer illusion, the results of varying the length and inclination of the arms are of some interest. They are most conveniently observed by using the arrow head and feather head figures in separate experiments, one or other of them being each time exhibited with a simple horizontal line for comparison. As the arms are lengthened in either figure, the illusion increases up to a certain point, beyond which further lengthening of the arms produces diminution in the size of the illusion. The smaller the angles which the arms form with the

horizontal, the shorter is the length of the arms at
which the point of maximal illusion is reached.
Further, the amount of the maximal illusion diminishes, as we might expect, as the angles formed by
the arms with the horizontal increase. Indeed with
the feather head figure, the illusion becomes reversed
when the angles exceed 60 degrees, and the arms are
short. Under these conditions the illusion resembles
in nature *EF* (fig. 6) which appears shorter than *YZ*
unless the arms are relatively long (e.g. exceeding
half the length of the horizontal line). In this figure

Fig. 6.

the arms tend to restrict the apparent size of the
whole. The same explanation of the illusion is available as before ; we unconsciously take into account
the entire figure when estimating the length of a
part.

Figure 6 may be taken as a geometrically limiting
case of the Müller-Lyer illusion. The other limiting
case is, of course, figure 7, where, as in the feather
head illusion, the end arms cause the line *GH* to
appear longer than *YZ*. The same explanation is
applicable to this figure. The subject always tends
to be influenced by the size of the whole figure,
especially in this case where the whole figure is of

the same nature as its part, namely a horizontal line. There is thus every inducement for him to attribute to a part *GH* the length of the whole, and consequently *GH* appears longer than it would otherwise appear.

As the terminal arms beyond *G* and *H* are increased in length until each measures about three-fifths of the central line, the illusion increases (as in the Müller-Lyer illusion) but beyond this point it diminishes and finally reverses. This increase of the illusion with increasing length of the arms proves

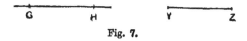

Fig. 7.

that the interaction is one not between one part, *GH* and other parts, the two end pieces, but between a part and the whole of the figure. The same fact is indicated by the length of the arms at the point of reversal. Evidently here we have two influences at work. When the arms are relatively short, the subject confuses the length of the part with the whole. As the arms lengthen, there is an increasing tendency to contrast the length of the part with that of the whole. We may call these two antagonistic factors 'confluxion' and 'contrast.' Confluxion consists in a diminution, contrast in an exaggeration, of the difference between part and whole.

These two factors, confluxion and contrast, may be regarded as the basis of the Müller-Lyer illusion. So long as the arms are relatively short, confluxion

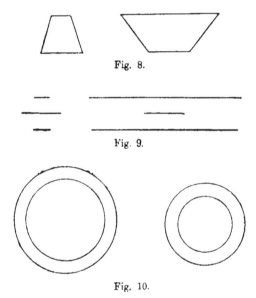

Fig. 8.

Fig. 9.

Fig. 10.

predominates; as the arms lengthen, contrast comes more and more to the fore.

The effects of confluxion are well seen in the above three pairs of figures 8, 9 and 10. In figure 8 the

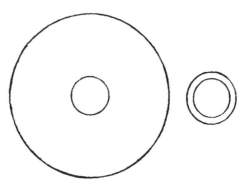

Fig. 11.

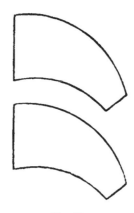

Fig. 12.

bases, in figure 9 the middle lines are actually of equal length; in figure 10, the inner circle of the left-hand figure is equal to the outer circle of the right-hand figure.

The effects of contrast are shown in the following pairs of figures. In fig. 11 the inner circles, in fig. 12

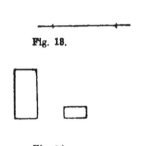

Fig. 18.

Fig. 14.

the entire figures are of exactly the same size (the contrast in the latter is between the adjoining curves of the two figures); in fig. 13 the middle portions of the two lines, in fig. 14 the bases are of equal length.

CHAPTER IV

MUCH of the modern work in the field of Aesthetics
lies clearly within the scope of Experimental Psychology. Investigations have been conducted in very
different ways. The first of those which we shall
mention consists in accurately observing and analyzing
the material that is used for aesthetic purposes.
What forms of curve, what proportions of length
to breadth, what combinations of colour are most
frequently used in architecture, sculpture, drawing
and painting? What are the intervals and rhythms
which are employed in music? Answers to such
questions may be expected to elucidate the principles that underlie the construction of works of
art, and to determine the extent to which these
principles have varied within a given community
from time to time and among different communities
according to their social environment.

In the comparative study of music, the phonograph
has proved of striking value in fixing the intervals

and rhythms actually used by different peoples in their music. This instrument has a diaphragm consisting of a thin glass disc to whose under surface a sharp sapphire point is attached. The point can be made to cut a spiral groove in the wax surface of a rotating cylinder. When the diaphragm is thrown into vibration by the voice of the singer or by the notes of the instrument played before it, the sapphire point cuts marks into the wax which vary according to the pitch, the loudness, the number and the sequences of the tones of which the music is composed. The record, once made, can be reproduced by substituting a disc provided with a blunt glass point in place of the sharp sapphire one. When the blunt point is introduced into the already cut grooves of the rotating wax cylinder, it is thrown into vibration, and the glass diaphragm with which it is connected is also thrown into vibration; these vibrations, being communicated to the air, thus become manifest to the listener. In order to reproduce the actual pitch of the notes originally sung into the phonograph, it is essential that the cylinder rotates at the same rate when reproducing as when recording the music. This is easily secured by sounding a note of known pitch (from a tuning-fork or a pitchpipe) before the phonograph when the record is being taken, and by altering the speed of revolution during reproduction until this note has the same pitch as it had when sounded before the phonograph. The faster the cylinder revolves, the higher will be the pitch of the notes which it reproduces. The intervals, however, are always constant.

In listening to a tune thus reproduced by the phonograph, it is easy to prevent the glass point from travelling onward while the cylinder is rotating. It may be made to slip back into the same groove instead of travelling onward along the continuous spiral cut in the wax surface. By this means any one note in the tune may be prolonged at will and so its pitch may be ascertained with considerable accuracy.

To determine the pitch of the tones emitted by the phonograph, it is convenient to use for purposes of comparison an instrument which yields a great number of tones successively differing only by two vibrations. Such an instrument is Appun's *Tonmesser*, which consists of a series of metal tongues enclosed in a case and blown by bellows. Any one tongue can be sounded at will by pulling out the stop which is connected with it. The pitch of each note of the *Tonmesser* being accurately known, it is easy to pull out one stop after another until a pitch is reached which coincides exactly with that of the note meanwhile being emitted from the phonograph.

The rhythms used by some peoples, especially in playing primitive instruments of percussion, are apt to be extraordinarily complex,—so complex indeed, that they defy analysis by the unaccustomed European ear. Rhythm, however, like pitch can be fixed by mechanical means and investigated later under convenient conditions in the laboratory. The musician is provided with an instrument resembling a drum but so modified that each beat on it momentarily closes an electric current or pulls on a cord. The closure of the current or the tension of the cord actuates a lever the point of which writes on a rotating cylinder covered with smoked paper. Below this lever is another lever which regularly marks, say, each fifth of a second on the rotating cylinder. Thus at each drum beat the upper lever is momentarily depressed, while the lower is depressed at each fifth of a second. The paper on the rotating cylinder is subsequently removed from the drum and varnished. A careful examination of the relation between the upper and lower series of marks will fix the time interval between successive beats and will yield the principle on which the complex rhythm of the drum beats is founded.

This procedure, adopted in the comparative study of music, will serve to illustrate the 'method of observation,' in which note is taken of the material actually employed in aesthetics. Various other methods, however, are at our command. We may employ the 'method of absolute judgment,' in which a subject is asked to pronounce an opinion on each member of a series of successively given objects (e.g. rectangles, curves, colours or tones, exposed singly or in combination, according to the purpose of the experiment). He may be required to give his judgment in the terms 'very pleasant,' 'pleasant,' 'indifferent,' 'unpleasant,' 'very unpleasant,' or, in similar grades, in terms of beauty and ugliness.

The experimenter may proceed by noting the different judgments given by different individuals and by obtaining so far as possible from each the reasons for their judgments. The question, 'Is this colour pleasant or unpleasant, and for what reason?', has disclosed some interesting differences in the 'aspect' of colour which appeals to different people, i.e., in the attitude which they naturally adopt towards colour. One aspect has been termed 'objective.' The individual who looks at colour from the objective aspect, judges of a colour according as it comes up to or falls short of his standard for that colour. He likes, let us say, a certain red because it is fully saturated, dislikes a green because it has too much yellow in it. Another aspect has been termed 'physiological.' A colour is liked because it produces a warm, stimulating effect on him ; it is disliked because it is depressing or glaring to his eyes. A third aspect is the 'associative.' A red is disliked because it reminds him of blood ; a certain green is liked because it recalls the dress of a certain person. Lastly, there is the 'character' aspect, in which colours are individualised, and given the peculiarities of persons. One colour is honest, another jealous, a third melancholy ; other colours appear underhand, treacherous, good-natured, laughing, stately, playful, flippant, and so on.

Similar aspects hold for colour-combinations and for tones and tone-combinations. A tone or chord is disliked because it is 'not quite what it ought to be' (objective aspect), or it is liked because it rouses the subject to 'a pleasant sense of alertness' (physiological aspect). It may be liked because it recalls the opening phrase of a piece of music of which the subject is fond (associative aspect), or because it is gentle or fearless (character aspect). These various aspects no doubt influence our appreciation of the beautiful.

In all forms of art, elements which are not beautiful in themselves become aesthetically valuable in relation to the whole. A dull colour may enhance the beauty of a neighbouring colour ; a discord may even be liked for its connexions with the preceding and following sounds. But the complex conditions which arise when elementary units are grouped into higher units should not discourage the investigation of the aesthetic effects of the simpler units when isolated from any context. It is only by experimenting with simple material that we can hope to progress towards the understanding of the complex conditions of everyday life. In all fields of knowledge abstract study within the laboratory precedes investigations in applied science. The special value of simple material lies in the fact that we are able to vary it in any direction (size, hue, brightness, loudness) we please, and can thus investigate the effects of these influences separately.

Another method of procedure is the 'choice method.' Here the subject actively selects from a number of objects (colours, forms, etc.) that which is most pleasing or beautiful, or he ranges them all in order according to the pleasure or aesthetic experience which they yield him. This in large measure involves comparative judgments and is less reliable thar other methods of comparison, of which the following is an example.

In this method pairs of objects are exposed, a judgment being pronounced on each, until each member of the series has been compared with every other member. *A* is given with *B*, *A* with *C*, *A* with *D* and so on. But if a judgment is obtained when *A* lies to the left of or precedes *B*, we must also enquire into the judgment that results when *A* lies to the right of or follows *B*. The influence of arrangement in space and time evidently has great influence on our judgment. Thus *B* must be given with *A*, *C*, *D*, etc., and then *C* with *A*, *B*, *D*, etc., and so on, until a complete series of judgments has been obtained.

We may also plan experiments so as to investigate special conditions influencing the aesthetic judgment. The objects may be exposed for different periods of time, in order to trace the influence of duration on the waxing and waning of the pleasure or displeasure afforded, and to study the various experiences of the subject during exposure. The same object may be shown at different times to the same subject, so as to determine the effects of familiarity, previous occupation, mood, etc. The same objects may be presented simultaneously now in one position, now in another relatively to each other, so as to show the influence of balance, symmetry and the like within a given space. The effect of different rhythms and combination of rhythms and the interpolation of pauses both in music and poetry have been experimentally investigated. But in all these lines of research, only the surface of the ground, so to speak, has been scratched. The conclusions drawn are too tentative and uncertain to be given here. But they are suggestive enough to make it certain that Aesthetics can never in the future neglect the experimental treatment of the subject.

Lastly it may be mentioned that the aesthetic experience may be studied in its relation to respiration and circulation by appropriate instruments. We are able to register variations in the depth and rate of breathing by means of the pneumograph, fig. 15. A simple form of this instrument consists of a metal cylinder closed at each end by rubber sheeting and provided with a side opening. A hook is attached to the surface of each rubber sheet. To one hook a piece of tape is attached which passes tightly round the chest of the subject, the other end of the tape being attached to the other hook. As the subject expands and contracts his chest, air is drawn into and driven out of the pneumograph. These move- ments of the air are communicated to a recording

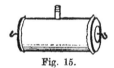

Fig. 15.

'tambour,' fig. 16, by a tube, one end of which is attached to the tambour, and the other to the side opening of the pneumograph. The lever of the tambour which thus moves up or down with every respiratory movement is brought to write on the travelling surface of a sheet of smoked paper.

The rate of the pulse and the form of the pulse curve may be studied by means of the sphygmograph applied to a superficial artery. The changes in arterial pressure are communicated by a system of delicate levers to a recording surface.

By means of these and other instruments we may determine to what extent the aesthetic judgment influences or is influenced by organic movements. Experiments have likewise been undertaken to determine whether voluntary movements determine the aesthetic judgment. It has been maintained on insufficient evidence that the speed of rhythm most preferred depends on the individual's natural rate of walking. It has been suggested that the eye's

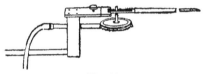

Fig. 16.

appreciation of beauty in a vase is dependent on the agreeable sensations obtained from the movements of the eyes as they sweep over the curves of its outline. But introspection shows that the sensations obtained from the eye movements are comparatively unimportant, and photography has demonstrated that the eyes wander in an irregular zig-zag fashion when they regard the graceful outlines of an object.

CHAPTER V

PAST experiences tend to recur spontaneously. We well know how if we have heard a 'catchy' tune, or if we have seen a man run over, the experience is apt to repeat itself in the mind during the next few hours or days. So too, when tired, e.g., just before going to sleep, we often review the most striking of recent events. This tendency of past experiences to reproduce themselves spontaneously is to psychologists known as 'perseveration.' We shall presently see how it may be studied experimentally. Experiment has shown that perseveration varies greatly according to the individual and according to his state of fatigue, the nature of the original experience, and the time elapsing since it occurred.

When an experience is thus revived, it may appear in exactly its original form, except for a diminution in clearness and vividness. But here again experiment has shown a very wide difference among individuals. There are some people who so vividly see in their 'mind's eye' objects which are recalled, that they appear in their original colours. There are others whose visual imagery is less pronounced. Though unable or rarely able to visualise colours, they distinctly visualise forms. In others imagery is most pronounced for sounds or movements, or for tastes or smells. There are others, again, in whom one or more of these various forms of imagery is almost if not completely lacking. To them it seems ridiculous to talk of seeing forms and colours or of hearing sounds or of feeling their own movements in memory. They recall experiences as a rule in terms not of concrete objects but of words. These individuals, who make such frequent use of verbal imagery, vary again in the degree to which they see the words, hear them, or articulate them 'in their mind'; here, again, that is to say, three varieties of imagery, visual, auditory and motor, play different parts according to the individual. Finally there is experimental and other evidence that revival is possible in the absence of any form of imagery whatever. That is to say, past experiences may be remembered not in the form of imagery, but as imageless thoughts.

Such individual differences have long been the subject of psychological investigation. Their importance is obvious in regard to heredity, education, practice, and occupation in life. In order to conduct experiments on imagery and indeed on memory generally, which shall be comparable among different individuals, it is usually desirable that the material which is to be revived shall be as simple as possible. For this purpose letters, figures, or three-letter syllables are commonly employed; and special care is taken to avoid as far as possible any suggestion of meaning, so that the material shall have the same interest among different individuals.

If different subjects learn, say, a row of twelve letters for the same time and be tested after an equal interval, it is curious to observe what different methods are used in learning and what different errors occur during attempted reproduction of the letters, according to the imagery of the individual. Other things being equal, the person who has pronounced visual imagery learns best by seeing the letters; he who has pronounced auditory or motor imagery learns the letters best while hearing or articulating them. When tested after learning, the visualiser makes mistakes of memory by substituting letters of like form; he will return an *O* for a *C*. Those in whom auditory imagery is specially developed will confuse letters of like sound, e.g. returning *S* for *C*. The former 'type' *sees* the letters, the latter *hears* them, a third, the motor type, experiences a tendency to *utter* them during reproduction.

Two well-known 'lightning calculators' were examined for their imagery in this way. One of them was found to be a very striking example of the visual, the other of the auditory type. The one was able to re-present an entire card of figures in his mind's eye, so that he could without effort reproduce them diagonally or in whatever order desired. This the other calculator could only do with the utmost difficulty; he hardly visualised the figures at all, but reproduced them successively by means of auditory imagery.

Perseveration, the tendency of experiences to recur spontaneously, is obviously not the sole or most important condition of revival. Experiences tend to reproduce themselves also by virtue of their association one with another. Psychologists have come to speak of a 'strong' or a 'weak' association between two earlier consecutive experiences a and b, according to the tendency possessed by a, when subsequently re-exhibited, to revive b. In such a case, from the standpoint of experiment, the association may be spoken of as 'wholly constrained'; only *one* reply returned by the subject can be correct.

But under other circumstances the association may be 'free'; e.g., the subject may be asked to give the *first idea which occurs to him* when a is exhibited, a being a word, sentence, picture, colour, sound, according to the conditions of experiment. By means of appropriate apparatus, it is easy to measure the interval elapsing between the exhibition of a and the subject's response. Such intervals are called 'association times.' These vary in length according to the individual, his condition and the nature of the stimulus a. If the stimulus finds connexion with a past experience of the subject which was attended with much emotional disturbance, the association time is apt to be very much prolonged. Indeed very often association experiments appear to have successfully played the part of a detective agency. A series of words is prepared by the experimenter, including some which have more or less obscure reference to the crime of which the subject is suspected, or to the thoughts he is supposed to be more or less sub-consciously harbouring. The association times for the various words are compared and turn out as a rule to be appreciably longer for the words which relate to the repressed conditions. Thus if several subjects be tested, one of whom is suspected, say, of having stolen a rare book from a certain library, the thief would give longer association times than the others when such words were exhibited as had reference to the theft, alluding, for instance, to the rarity, title or contents of the book, the shelf, and so on. The test, however, could not be expected to succeed, where the thief is absolutely callous or where an innocent person knows that he is suspected of the theft.

Under other experimental conditions, the association may be 'partially constrained.' The subject may
be asked to give an epithet, or a specific or generic
instance, suited to the noun exhibited, to give an
idea connecting two words simultaneously exhibited,
or even to give a report on an object, a picture, or a
sentence placed before him. Thus by a series of steps
we may advance in experimenting through imagery
and association to the study of thought itself.

Turning to the classification of associations, we
find that the associations which are due to similarity
of form and to similarity of meaning are the two
most fundamental varieties. If the word *stye* or *file*
is returned when the word *stile* is exhibited, the
association is almost certainly of the first variety.
If the word *step*, *gate* or *field* is returned, the
association is almost certainly of the second. Association by meaning may involve either 'abstract' or
'concrete' thought, 'reproductive' or 'constructive'
imagination, and so on. Experiments have been
conducted with the object of investigating how age,
sex, fatigue, drugs and mental disorders affect the
relative frequency of these varieties of association.

Let us return now to that form of association, the
'wholly constrained' association, which is of special
interest in relation to memory. Here, it will be
remembered, there can only be one correct reply to
the word which is exhibited ; *a* is shown to the

subject, b must be returned by him. In experiments on memory a and b are learnt together. A certain strength of association is built up between them. This strength can be measured experimentally by determining (i) the length of time elapsing after a is given, before b is reproduced, (ii) the success with which b is reproduced. Clearly if the association is weak, a fails to revive b; if it be stronger, a slowly recalls b; if it be very strong, b is reproduced with much less delay.

In actual experiment, however, it is impossible to measure the strength of a *single* association. The average reproduction time and the average 'score' (as we may call the successful reproductions of b) are deduced from a number of pairs a—b, c—d, e—f, g—h, which are learnt together on the same occasion. For example, a series of twelve meaningless syllables,

nus, kar, tuf, jis, reb, woj,
saf, gep, moz, huk, bim, tad,

is read off in pairs by the subject. By accentuating the first of every pair, he learns them in trochaic rhythm. While reading them he sits before a screen, and the experimenter successively brings the various syllables before an opening in the screen at a measured rate, so that each syllable is exhibited for the same length of time and has the chance of

receiving an equal measure of attention during
learning. When the experimenter has exhibited
the twelve syllables once, he immediately exhibits
them again and again. Thus the subject reads the
entire series a number of times, the number being
determined by the experimenter but always being
insufficient to effect a perfect reproduction. Then
without, or after, a pause the subject's memory is
tested. The accented syllables, *reb*, *bim*, *nus*, etc.,
are successively exhibited by the experimenter in
quite irregular order. A time-registering apparatus
is set going at the moment of exhibition of each of
these syllables, the apparatus being so arranged that
it records in thousandths of seconds the length of
interval elapsing between the exhibition of the accented syllable and the reply of the subject. After
response has been made to one accented syllable,
another is exhibited. When the subject replies
correctly, it is counted as a score ; when he replies
wrongly or fails to reply, it is counted as a miss.
The time taken to effect a score is called the 'scoring
time.' Consequently such an experiment of incompletely learning a series of twelve syllables gives two
sets of measurements, the percentage of scores and
the average scoring time.

It is at once evident what a variety of experiments
can be studied by means of this 'scoring method.'
We may study the effects of decreasing or increasing

(i) the number of the syllables in the series, (ii) the number of repetitions allowed for reading, (iii) the rate of reading, (iv) the effects of accent, (v) the duration of the pause between reading and testing. There are many other investigations which have been worked out by this and other methods of experiments. Into the most important results of these we shall now enter.

It has been found that the most marked lapse of memory occurs immediately after learning. When associations which are ten minutes old (i.e., when an interval of ten minutes is allowed to elapse between reading and testing) are compared with associations which have only just been formed, there is a far greater difference in the number of scores than when associations which are twenty-four hours old are compared with those which are ten minutes old. No doubt the specially favourable factor in the case of just acquired association is perseveration. Perseveration, as we all know, is most effective in 'immediate' memory. Those in whom it is most marked are able to depend more on learning mechanically than on learning rationally, i.e. with the help of meaning. The actor who contrives to become word-perfect in his part after a few hours' notice, the boy who 'crams' his lesson just before his class meets, are well-known instances of the condition in which rational learning plays a very

small part, perseveration is the predominant factor,—
and memory quickly fails immediately after learning.

Apart, however, from this loss due to the waning
of perseveration, the time elapsing between learning
and reproduction has to a certain extent a favourable
effect, in that it allows of the 'consolidation' of
associations. Everyone must have observed that a
lesson incompletely learnt at night may be perfectly
reproducible in the morning. Experiment has shown
that, when an association c—d is learnt after an
association a—b has been formed, the formation of
c—d tends to diminish the strength of a—b. This
'retro-active inhibition, as it is called, disappears in
the course of time, so that a certain improvement in
the strength of the first-learnt association then occurs.
We may thus explain the fact that if a series of
syllables be learnt and tested a few minutes after
learning, a smaller number of scores and of short
scoring times is obtainable than when a series of
like difficulty is learnt and is tested after a somewhat longer interval since learning.

Indeed from the following experimental result it
appears that perfect rest after learning is the best
means of removing the effects of retro-active inhibition. Four series of twelve syllables, which we
may term A, were read eight times by the subject
who thereupon, before being tested, proceeded to
examine a set of three pictures closely enough to be

able to undergo a catechism as to their contents. Four like series of twelve syllables, which we may term B, were read a like number of times, but the like interval between learning and testing was made as restful as possible. The percentage scores for A and B turned out to be 24 and 56, the averaging scoring times 2·95 and 2·49 secs., respectively.

In another method of learning, called the 'saving method,' senseless syllables are prepared as before, but after each reading the subject attempts to reproduce the series, and the readings are continued until a completely successful reproduction has been effected. A given interval, prescribed by the experimenter, is allowed to elapse ; whereupon the subject again alternately reads and tries to reproduce the series until he has completely learnt them. The economy in time or the number of repetitions saved on the second occasion as compared with the first, is taken as a measure of the average association strength of that series in the subject before re-learning.

By the use of the scoring method, it has been experimentally shown that material is better retained in memory when the repetitions are spread over a considerable period of time than when they are accumulated at a single sitting. This cannot be explained as being due to the greater fatigue or loss of interest involved in accumulated readings. For when a subject learnt one series of syllables, A, by twenty-four repetitions equally distributed over three days, a second series B by twenty-four repetitions distributed over six days, and a third series C by twenty-four repetitions distributed over twelve days (the three series being tested respectively on the fourth, seventh and thirteenth days, and due regard being paid to an equal amount of learning being done on successive days), A was found to give 7 scores, B 31 scores, and C 55 scores. Here differences of fatigue and interest could not have been of importance, as the conditions in B and C only differed by two readings daily. Nor can the results be attributed to the involuntary recall of syllables during the intervals between repetition, for similar results have been obtained where minutes instead of days have separated the groups of repetitions from one another.

There is reason to believe that the superior efficacy of the most distributed readings is primarily due to the fact that when two associations are of like strength but of unlike age, repetition has a greater effect in increasing the strength of the older than of the younger association. That is to say, other things being equal, an older association is more rapidly strengthened by repetition than a younger. The following experiment, complicated though it is, is worth citing in confirmation of this statement.

A subject reads two series of twelve syllables, which we will call A_1, A_1', thirty times. The experimenter tests the subject's memory for these series twenty-four hours later, employing the saving method for one series, the scoring method for the other. After this test, the subject at once reads two new syllable series, which we will call B_1, B_1', four times. One minute after the last reading of each, one is tested by the saving, the other by the scoring method. Then two fresh series, A_2, A_2', are read thirty times. Twenty-four hours later, the series A_2, A_2', are tested, one by the saving, the other by the scoring method, after which two series B_2, B_2' are read four times and tested as B_1, B_1' were, and two series A_3, A_3' are read thirty times. So the research continues for twenty-one days, on each day (save the first) four series being read and four being tested. Sometimes the test by the saving method precedes, at other times it follows, that by the scoring method; and other precautions are taken so that the conditions remain as uniform as possible. The following are the results obtained—

	Average number of repetitions to re-learn by saving method	Average percentage score	Average scoring time
Series A	5·85	9	4·503 secs.
Series B	9·60	27	1·725 secs.

Now the experiment has been so planned that

the associations in the *A* series are twenty-four hours
old, while those in the *B* series are one minute old
when they are tested. The scores and scoring times
given above show as might be expected that the
association strength is much greater in series *B*
than in series *A*. On the other hand, many more
repetitions are required to re-learn the *B* series than
to re-learn the *A* series. Let us now suppose that
the experiment had been so planned that the series
A had been read more than thirty times and the
series *B* had been read less than four times. Under
such conditions the average scores and scoring times of
the twenty-four hours old and one minute old associations might have been approximately equal. Obviously
series *A* would have then required a still fewer, and
series *B* a still greater number of repetitions than is
given above in order that they might be re-learnt by
the saving method. No doubt there are various
factors (e.g. perseveration tendencies) which complicate
the issue here. These, however, are not of sufficient
influence to invalidate the conclusion that when two
associations have the same strength but are of unequal
age, repetitions have a greater effect on the older
than on the younger association.

Both the saving and the scoring methods have
been used to investigate whether learning a given
task by reading it completely through time after
time is more economical than learning it section by

section until the whole has been learnt. It appears
that the method of 'entire' learning is the more
favourable, the difference being more marked, the
greater be the number of sections into which the task
is divided in the method of 'sectional' learning.
Even a 'mixed' method, which is the one natural
perhaps to most persons,—where although the task
is learnt in sections the matter is recited from the
beginning after each section has been learnt,—is
inferior to the method of entire learning so far as
retention is concerned. Even, too, when the task
consists of very unfamiliar words, it is better retained
by the entire method of learning, although the
number of repetitions may be greater here than by
the sectional methods of learning. As, however,
individuals differ in respect of perseveration tendency
and in liability to what we have called retro-active
inhibition, only a general statement of this kind
is possible. A strong perseveration tendency may
perhaps be expected to favour the method of sectional
learning, while weak retro-active inhibition may be
expected to favour the method of entire learning.
The latter method allows the subject to form a
general impression of the whole task and to gain
increasing familiarity with the meaning at each
reading. Success, however, appears remote and the
subject is apt to feel discouraged. In the method
of sectional learning, on the other hand, the subject

is stimulated by accomplishing the learning of section after section. But he forms unnecessary associations, which later have to be annulled, between the end and the beginning of any one section ; and his attention is apt to wander during the successive repetitions of the same section.

When a series of syllables *a, b, c, d*, etc., is read through time after time, there is evidence that not only are 'direct' associations formed between *a* and *b, b* and *c*, etc., but that 'remote' associations are also formed, between *a* and *c*, between *b* and *d*, between *a* and *d*, etc., and 'retro-active' associations, between *b* and *a, c* and *b*, and even between *d* and *b, c* and *a*, etc. Experiments have been conducted in the following manner. Six series, each of sixteen syllables, are learnt, and on the following day six series derived therefrom are learnt. The saving of time is noted by the saving method. The derived series are prepared in one of the following seven ways,—(i) by omitting alternate syllables, (ii) by omitting two, (iii) by omitting three, (iv) by omitting seven consecutive syllables, (v) by reversing the order of the syllables in the series, (vi) by reversing the order and omitting alternate syllables, (vii) by arranging the syllables in haphazard order, with the exception of the first and the last. The last method of preparation was devised to prove that mere familiarity with the syllables of the original series could not account for the saving in learning the derived series. The results may be conveniently expressed in the following table—

Method	Percentage of time saved in learning the derived series
(i)	10·8
(ii)	7·0
(iii)	5·8
(iv)	3·3
(v)	12·0
(vi)	5·0
(vii)	0·5

We see that when a series is learnt, a vast number of subsidiary associations are formed besides the principal associations. What is learnt forms a whole, the parts of which are linked or knitted together in all directions. This knitting together of the parts to form a whole proceeds from the two ends of the series towards the middle ; as can be demonstrated by noting the frequency of errors or gaps in trying to reproduce a partially learnt series. The errors are more numerous in the middle, the successes at the ends, of the series.

A series of seven syllables can be apprehended as a unitary whole by an expert learner during a single recital. The following table shows the average number of repetitions required to learn series of syllables of different length. They hold, of course,

only for the person who formed the subject of the
investigation—

Number of syllables in series	7	12	16	24	86
Number of repetitions needed	1	16·6	30	44	55

We have a good deal of evidence to show that
when a given association a—c is acquired after the
laying down of an association a—b, the latter is not
annihilated. It is only inhibited for the time being.
Indeed other things being equal, the older association
is found to outlast the younger. Many instances of
this principle will readily occur to the reader.

The knitting together of simpler into more
complex units, in which the learning of a task
essentially consists, is of course far easier in the
case of sensible than in the case of senseless material.
Senseless syllables can be linked together only by
virtue of their association in time and space, but
the learning of sensible material involves also the
influence of meaning. By virtue of meaning, a group
of words or a short phrase immediately becomes a
unit. It is no wonder then how much more easily
sensible matter is learnt and retained. One investigator, for example, finds that, whereas a series
of thirty-six senseless syllables requires fifty-five
repetitions, he can learn in eight repetitions a stanza
of Byron's *Don Juan*, which contains about eighty

syllables in thirty-six words when articles, prepositions and similar dependent words are left out of account.

Even senseless syllables are apt to possess some meaning for the learner. And at the outset the novice is apt to use every effort to remember them by the aid of mnemonics. But with increasing practice such help is discarded. He comes to rely solely on mechanical memory. All unnecessary thoughts and movements, all the variations in direction of attention—now to the rhythm of recital, now to the position of the syllables, now to one or another form of imagery—cease as the subject becomes more expert. He concentrates himself more and more on solely impressing the material.

Those who excel in such mechanical memory are usually endowed with strong perseveration tendencies or with very powerful imagery. Such qualities, of course, naturally favour learning for immediate reproduction,—immediate memory, as it is called. But, as we have pointed out, rational learning in the end results in far better retention than mechanical learning. The former, of course, involves the latter, with the addition to it of meaning.

CHAPTER VI

MENTAL TESTS AND THEIR USES

WE use the word 'mental' in the broadest sense. At first sight it may appear erroneous to apply this epithet to some of the tests described in this chapter. But closer examination will show that they all involve, in varying degree, such processes as interpretation, judgment or, at least, volition, and that all are consequently of immediate interest for the psychologist.

Sensory acuity. The following useful test for visual acuity will serve as an instance. A number of *E*'s are printed in different positions on a circular card (fig. 17). This card is covered by another, bearing eccentrically a small round window and capable of being rotated so that any particular *E* is displayed to the subject according to the wish of the experimenter who holds the card before the subject. The test is most satisfactorily conducted out-of-doors, preferably on a dull cloudy day (although in point of fact, differences of illumination, such as occur out-of-doors, have comparatively little influence on the

result). The subject first stands at a distance
from the card at which he can distinguish without
difficulty the form of the letter. He holds in his
hand a large cardboard model of an *E* and he is
asked to place his *E* in the same position as that of
the letter displayed in the window of the test card.
Ten trials should be made in order to be sure that
the subject understands what is required of him,

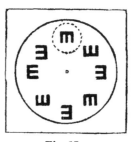

Fig. 17.

especially if he be a child or an illiterate person;
the great advantage of this test being that it does
not involve a previous knowledge of letters and is
thus applicable to all sorts and conditions of mankind. Then the subject is moved two metres[1] further
away from the card and ten tests are again made.
If he succeeds, the distance is again increased by two
metres and he is again tested, and so on until he

---

[1] See footnote to p. 33 for corresponding British measure.

begins to make mistakes in placing the *E*. Perhaps
he makes one error in ten trials, and corrects it.
Then the distance is increased by one metre, and if
he now makes not more than two errors in ten trials,
this distance is taken as the measure of his visual
acuity.

Even in so simple a test as this, it is impossible
to avoid complications arising from the entrance,
in different degrees in different subjects, of higher
mental processes. One subject will only place his *E*
in the required position when he clearly sees the *E*
displayed to him. Another will readily recognise the
possibility of interpreting the true position of the
letter at distances at which he sees it very indistinctly.
The letter may appear to him a mere blur, but nevertheless a faint gap or some vague difference in
outline may suffice to suggest that the open end of
the letter lies to the right or left, or upwards or
downwards. Some individuals are especially prone
to make use of such inferences, while others seem
naturally incapable of profiting by them.

The letter usually employed in this test is of such
a size that it can be read at a distance of six metres
by people who are credited with so-called 'normal'
vision. Such a person's visual acuity is described as
being $\frac{6}{6}$. Those who can read the letter at twelve
or eighteen metres are said to have a visual acuity
of $\frac{12}{6}$ or $\frac{18}{6}$; while the visual acuity of those who

can only read the letter at four or at two metres'
distance is expressed as $\frac{4}{6}$ or $\frac{2}{6}$, respectively. We
may of course represent the visual acuity (V) of these
four values as 2, 3, $\frac{2}{3}$, $\frac{1}{3}$, i.e., as equivalent to twice,
thrice, two-thirds, and one-third the so-called normal
acuity.

The tales which have so frequently been told by
travellers about the marvellous acuity of vision
among primitive peoples unquestionably depend, not
on a vastly superior visual acuity, but on the power
of interpreting signs which are meaningless to the
European and hence escape his notice. For when
the E test which we have just described is applied
to primitive folk, the results show a visual acuity
which is not very different from, though perhaps on
the whole slightly superior to, the acuity of Europeans
living a corresponding out-of-door life. The following
table will suffice to show the order of these differences
in two peoples whose average acuity is somewhat
better than that of a European community similarly
tested—

	Number tested	Average acuity	V=1 to 1	V=1·2 to 2	V=2·1 to 3	V=3·1 to 4
Torres Straits and Fly River, New Guinea	170	2·12	8·8	35·9	51·8	3·5%
Todas, Madras	98	2·20	3·1	34·7	60·2	2·0%
Heligoland	100	1·76	14·0	56·0	30·0	0 %

Now and again, individuals have been examined
whose acuity even exceeds four times the so-called

normal, and it may be that such cases, rare as they are, are somewhat commoner among primitive than among civilised peoples. On the other hand, considerable differences may exist among different peoples in the frequency of hypermetropia, myopia and astigmatism. For this reason the visual acuity may be sometimes lowered, even when such defects are remedied with glasses, as it is often impossible to correct quite successfully defects due to errors of refraction.

Sensory discrimination. As a matter of fact every test of sensibility involves sensory discrimination ; the subject having in practice to discriminate between the experiences of a just perceptible and of an imperceptible or absent stimulus, for example, between darkness and the feeblest visible light or between silence and the faintest audible sound. But we are here applying the term to determinations of the just appreciable difference between two perceptible stimuli. We shall illustrate this form of test by describing a method of determining the just appreciable difference of pitch.

The most convenient source of sound is provided either by twanging two stretched wires, or by sounding two tuning-forks. The pitch of one of the wires or forks is kept constant. The pitch of the other is changed by means of a sliding clamp which in the case of the wire shortens the latter's length by a known amount, and in the case of the fork is moved up and down one of its prongs and can be firmly fixed at any position, the prong being graduated to scale. The forks are best sounded by being hit on the experimenter's knee and then applied to one ear of the subject. The actual difference in pitch between the two wires or forks at given positions of the clamp is easily ascertainable by sounding the two simultaneously and counting the frequency of the beats between them. Thus if three beats per second are heard, the difference in pitch between the two sounds amounts to three vibrations per second.

In experimentally determining the smallest perceptible difference of pitch, the tones are sounded before the subject successively not simultaneously, the duration of each tone and the interval between them each amounting to about two seconds. The subject is seated so that he cannot see the manipulations of the experimenter. Both the experimenter and the subject require some preliminary practice, the experimenter having to accustom himself to sounding the tones with constant loudness, and the subject, if he be un-musical or a savage, or child, having to understand clearly what is required of him. It is an advantage to put the subject through a preliminary test, in order roughly to find the interval which he cannot fail to appreciate and that which is too small for his appreciation.

The experimenter sounds the higher tone before the lower as often as the lower before the higher, and each time asks the subject to decide whether the second sound is lower or higher than the first, or whether both are of the same pitch. It is best to obtain five answers from the subject before the difference in pitch is changed. The experimenter starts with a difference which, from the preliminary test, he knows to be obvious to the subject. Having received five correct answers, he reduces the difference by a known amount and sounds the pairs of tones five times again. If he obtains five correct answers from the subject, he reduces the difference in pitch by the same amount again, and so on, until one error in five judgments is obtained. Then the same pair of tones is presented five times more and if another mistake is made, this pitch difference is taken as the minimal appreciable. Some experimenters continue still further to reduce the difference and then proceed by increasing the difference until again a point of just perceptible difference is reached.

The method has been applied with the object of discovering whether primitive peoples are more sensitive than ourselves to slight differences of pitch. Only one primitive community has thus been examined hitherto, but similar methods have been also used in different schools of this country.

Subjects	Number tested	Average Threshold	Extremes
Murray Islanders (Torres Straits) adults	16	15·4 vibr.	9 and 22 vibr.
Murray Islanders (Torres Straits) children	6	12·2 vibr.	8 and 19 vibr.
Aberdeenshire adults	19	7·6 vibr.	2 and 9 vibr.
Aberdeenshire school-children	10	10·6 vibr.	3 and 19 vibr.
An 'Elementary' school in Berkshire	24	9·8 vibr.	1·3 and 80 vibr.
An 'Elementary' school at Oxford	80	6·0 vibr.	1 and 11·5 vibr.
A 'Preparatory' school at Harrow	28	4·6 vibr.	0·6 and 20 vibr.
A 'Preparatory' school at Oxford	13	3·5 vibr.	0·3 and 8 vibr.

The first four results are quite comparable : the remaining four were obtained by two different observers, using somewhat different methods of experiment. We can see, however, that the sensitivity to difference of pitch is distinctly less among the adults of the primitive community than among those of civilised communities, and we have two indications that intelligence, education, and general culture are important factors in the test. For, despite the fact that the British Elementary school children had had fully as much previous training in music as those attending the Preparatory schools, the former prove less sensitive to pitch difference than the latter. And whereas the Murray Island and the Aberdeenshire adults differ enormously, there is very little difference between the school children of Aberdeenshire and those of Murray Island who are now being taught by a Scottish teacher.

A similar method of experiment may be used to arrive at the 'spatial threshold,' i.e. the smallest distance between two blunt compass points at which a double touch is appreciable when those points are simultaneously applied to the skin. But here it is advisable to introduce in addition an equal number of 'catch' experiments, viz., single point-touches, and, as the replies involve little fatigue, to increase the number of double touches to ten before the distance between the two points is reduced. The experimenter marks a point, say on the subject's forearm, in ink and this serves as the mid-point of the region to be explored. The subject closes his eyes and rests his arm comfortably on a table. As before, the experimenter allows the subject some preliminary practice in which to determine distances between the points which are clearly above and clearly below his spatial threshold. Then the compass points are separated by a distance wide enough to be perceptible to him as two, and ten double touches and ten single touches are made by the experimenter, in irregular order. If twenty correct answers are obtained, the distance is reduced by five millimetres and another set of twenty observations is taken. When two wrong answers in ten double touches have been obtained, this distance may be taken as the measure of the spatial threshold.

This experiment reveals the same individual differences in respect to interpretation as were brought to light in the test for visual acuity. When the two points are sufficiently near, a stage is reached when they are not felt as two but yet the touch seems different from a single-point touch. It appears more extended and blurred. Some individuals are found to make active use of this indication, whereas others will only state that they are touched by two points when the double touch is distinctly experienced as such. Such individual variation in behaviour, however, cannot be responsible for the remarkable differences in threshold which have been found among different peoples, as shown in the table on the following page.

It will be noticed that the Papuan Murray Islanders stand first on the list, having the lowest spatial threshold. They are able to distinguish a two-point from a one-point touch, when the compass points are separated by a distance of about a third of what is necessary in the case of the University men who stand at the opposite end of the list. Similarly, the boys at the Elementary school tend to be more sensitive to the test than those at the Preparatory school of the same age. (And an independent investigation undertaken at Tokio has shown that the same difference between Primary and Higher schools is to be found there.) Again, the Todas, who are unquestionably more cultured than the Papuans, fall between the latter and the Englishmen (when correction is made for the difference in method), while the Dayaks take their natural place between the Papuans and the Todas whose cultural level is not far removed from their own.

Subjects	Numbers tested	Average spatial threshold on forearm	Extremes
Murray Island, boys	25	14·0 mm.	2 and 25 mm.
Murray Island, men	50	19·8 mm.	2 and 40 mm.
Dayak, men	10	35 mm.	20 and 50 mm.
Toda, boys	6	*35 mm.	
Toda, men	28	*45·5 mm.	25 and 60 mm.
Oxford 'Elementary' school boys	80	36·2	19 and 58·3 mm.
Oxford 'Preparatory' school, boys	13	38·9	12·5 and 68·7 mm.
Aberdeenshire school children	18	*43	
Englishmen, mostly working men	23	44·6 mm.	10 and 90 mm.
Cambridge graduates and undergraduates	20	*56·5 mm.	40 and 70 mm.

* Owing to the employment of a slightly different experimental method, these figures should be reduced, roughly by 5 mm., in order that they may be strictly comparable to the rest.

One would have expected the peoples in this list to have stood in precisely the reverse order. One would have thought that the more intelligent and cultured the subject, the more ready would he be to employ to his advantage the slight differences between one- and two-point touches to which we have already alluded ; and the less liable would he show himself to the detrimental influences of distraction, carelessness and fatigue. There is some evidence that these several factors really have this expected action in advanced and primitive communities respectively. Probably therefore, if they could be excluded, the differences in threshold would be still more striking.

Just as difficult to understand as this decrease in tactile sensibility with increase of civilisation, is the discovery that the capacity to discriminate between lifted weights varies in the same sense, being greater among the more primitive than among the more civilised. There is no reason to suppose that primitive man has had more experience in discriminating touches and weights ; quite the contrary is probably true. We must be content, at present, merely with stating these results without venturing on an explanation of them. We have also to record that there is fair experimental evidence that the sensibility to pain is greater among civilised than among primitive peoples.

Motor Tests. In these tests we estimate the

amount, frequency and accuracy of bodily movement.
The amount may be roughly detected by the 'dyna-
mometer,' an instrument which the subject holds
between the palm and fingers of his hand and endeavours to squeeze as forcibly as possible. An index
with which the instrument is provided shows the
force which has been applied. Using another method,
the subject pulls his utmost against the resistance of
a steel spring, an index attached to which shows the
force exerted by the subject. The experiment may
be prolonged by enjoining the subject, blindfold,
to continue pulling at a maximum while a lever
connected with the index draws on a travelling
smoked surface a curve of the diminishing pull as
fatigue ensues.

Such methods, however, are extremely rough.
The record must vary with the way in which the
instrument is held, with the suddenness with which
the force is exerted, with the degree of pain and
discomfort thereby caused, and with the extent to
which auxiliary muscles are brought into play when
those at first used are becoming tired. Instead,
we prefer to use an instrument called the 'ergograph'
(fig. 18), in which the hand is comfortably but
securely held on a fixed platform F by means of the
clamps A and B. E is a box into which the middle
finger is inserted so as to fix its two terminal joints,
the index and ring fingers being separated from it by

Fig. 18.

the plates C and D. The hand and arm are thus fixed
so that only up and down movements of the middle
finger at the knuckle joint are possible. These movements are communicated to the spirally grooved
cylinder J by means of the steel ribbon H. To this
cylinder is attached a wire N which passes over a
pulley at the top of the board X, 10 feet or more in
height. The other end of the wire falls behind this

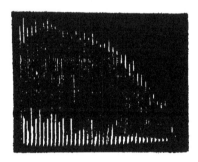

Fig. 19.

board and supports the weight W. To the same
cylinder is likewise attached a cord T which, passing
over two pulleys, records the extent of the up and
down movements of the finger by the lever L acting
against the spring L. Thus, every downward movement of the middle finger rotates the cylinder and
thereby raises the lever L and the weight W. The
total height to which the weight can be lifted (a

special arrangement prevents the weight falling during extension of the finger) when the finger is flexed to its maximum, say once every two seconds, indicates the total amount of work done before the muscle becomes totally exhausted. The up and down movements of the lever L can be studied by bringing it to bear on a slowly travelling smoked surface. Such an 'ergogram' is shown in fig. 19. We see that the movements start with wide excursions and soon diminish until the subject is wholly incapable of moving the finger at all.

Such ergograms have been obtained and compared under different conditions of work and fatigue. It has been shown that the ergogram varies widely in form according to the heaviness of the weight which has to be lifted. It has also been proved that the fatigue is only a special one ; that is to say, that there is only fatigue with respect to the particular weight which has been lifted. If the weight be slightly reduced, another ergogram can be immediately produced, equal to the former. Probably, indeed, we are to a large extent not dealing with fatigue at all. The condition of absolute impotence which gradually develops is perhaps in great part due to the effect of certain nervous impulses which ascend from the muscles of the finger to the spinal cord and the higher parts of the brain; these prevent, or, to use a common technical term, 'inhibit,' voluntary movement of that finger. At all events there is reason to believe that when owing to defects in the sensory apparatus, the usual muscular sensations of fatigue are impaired, muscular activity can be unduly prolonged. And we know that the ergogram is also favourably influenced by increased interest, pleasure or other mental excitement, which probably works by reducing or counteracting the 'inhibitory' effects of the nervous impulses just referred to.

Under conditions of well-marked mental fatigue, an unusually good ergogram is often obtainable. Here again we appear to have a reduction of that normal nervous control which usually guards the muscle from extreme exhaustion. So too many experimenters have noticed that at certain stages of its influence, alcohol causes an increased amount of muscular work, which, it is quite possible, may be capable of a similar explanation. The tendency of alcohol to weaken all inhibitory control and to increase general motor excitability at certain stages of its influence is well known outside the laboratory.

Alcohol, however, has a very complex effect on the intact organism. We know that in appropriate doses it acts on the excised muscle of the frog, at first increasing the amount of work and later diminishing it. There is some evidence that this action is due to effects on the nervous, rather than on the muscular, tissue of such a muscle-nerve preparation. In ourselves the taking of alcohol yields a pleasurable excitement and a definite sensory effect arising from stimulation of the mucous membrane of the stomach. If we are already accustomed to small or large doses of alcohol, there is likewise the effect of the satisfaction of a certain 'craving.' These factors, apart from the action of the drug on the nervous and muscular system, cannot fail to produce an effect on muscular work, as we have already observed. Indeed one observer has stated that alcohol may have a more marked effect when held in the mouth than when swallowed.

Such considerations are sufficient to show the extreme caution which must be employed in determining the effects of a drug on the human organism. Obviously the drug must in the first place be so disguised that the subject does not know that he is taking it. Two mixtures A and B must be prepared for him, equally pleasant (or unpleasant) to the taste, the one containing the drug, the other not. One of these mixtures is taken by the subject at each experiment, but throughout the investigation he must be ignorant which of the two mixtures contains the alcohol. Different strengths of the drug must be investigated. The work done on the days when the drug is taken must be compared, at the end, with that done on the days when the drug has not been taken. The effects of prolonged use of the drug have also to be compared with those of prolonged disuse. The effects of craving for the drug have to be eliminated by a preliminary period of prolonged abstinence. The immediate effects of the drug have to be compared with the later effects. In such a complex liquid as an alcoholic drink, the influence of the ethereal oils which it contains has to be worked out, besides the effect of the pure alcohol.

When the difficulties are so numerous, it is no wonder that conflicting results as to the action of alcohol on muscular work have been obtained. The most trustworthy investigations thus far recorded have been conducted in the following manner. Three sets, each of six ergograms, were obtained daily, an interval of two minutes between each ergogram being allowed for recovery, and an interval of half-an-hour elapsing between each set. The dose, whether of the disguised drug or of the control mixture, was not taken until after the first ergogram. In some experiments it was taken immediately upon the completion of the first ergogram; in others it was taken ten minutes before beginning the second set of ergograms. The order of the days on which the doses of the control mixture and those on which the different doses of alcohol in disguise were taken was unknown to the subject.

These investigations appear to show that small doses of pure alcohol, varying from 5 to 20 cubic

centimetres have no effect on the ergograms produced immediately or several hours afterwards. With
larger doses of 30 and 40 c.c. (the latter amount
being equivalent roughly to the alcohol contained in
a quarter of a tumbler of brandy) it was impossible to
disguise the factor of sensory stimulation entirely.
The effects were irregular; in some cases there
was no difference, in others a decrease or, perhaps
more commonly and especially at first, an increase
in the amount of work, as compared with the days on
which no alcohol was taken. That these irregular
results were not due to the methods employed is
shown by the evident effects which were brought to
light when such drugs as caffeine or strychnine were
substituted for the dose of alcohol.

In the case of caffeine, the effects of the drug on
the two subjects who were tested were manifestly
different. In both subjects there was an increased
capacity for work; but while in the one, it was so slight
that the question arose whether the increase was
greater than might result from mere accident, in
the other subject the influence of the drug was so
striking as to place it beyond all doubt. In the one
there was an initial increase which was soon followed
by a fall below the normal level; in the other the
effect was visible throughout the two sets of ergograms following the administration of the drug. In
the one subject the predominant effect of the drug

was to increase the height of the muscular contrac-
tions: in the other it was rather to increase their
number. There is some evidence that on the latter
subject the drug acted as an accelerator of fatigue.

The study of motor control can be readily studied
by such operations as card-dealing, type-writing or
simply by tapping. In the tapping or 'dot' test, a
strip of paper marked with a zig-zag row of small
circles arranged as in fig. 20 is rolled off, like the

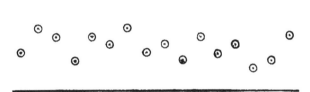

Fig. 20.

well-known Morse tape used in telegraph instruments,
from one spool on to another. By means of a suitable
slit, only a few spots are simultaneously visible at any
moment to the subject, who has to mark the centre of
each spot while they are passing before him. The
rate at which the strip is travelling can be varied at
will, but the clearest effects of fatigue are naturally
manifest when the speed is near the maximal rate for
the subject. Such an instrument serves to measure
the accuracy of the subject's aim and his ability to

sustain attention under various conditions. His success is evaluated by the number of dots he has marked and failed to mark in a given time. A drawback to such tests is that the unpractised subject is at first unfavourably influenced by muscular discomfort, and that when this has disappeared by training, the process of dotting becomes more and more mechanical. The latter disadvantage can however be obviated by varying the experiment, e.g. by asking the subject to mark every second or third, instead of each consecutive, dot. The evaluation of the results by this experiment is extremely laborious.

Simple arithmetical tests. These have for many years past been used as a test of mental work. Sheets of printed numbers are prepared and at a given signal the subject starts adding together successive pairs of figures, writing down the product in pencil at the side. The errors are negligible. A signal is given to the subject after the lapse of each minute, and he makes a mark beside the figures he is adding at the moment. It is possible to plot out a curve, showing the number of additions which have been performed during a given period for each consecutive minute. The method has thus been utilised for the study of improvability (i.e. the capacity to improve by practice), the retentiveness of improvement after varying pauses, fatigue, the relation of improvability to fatigability in different subjects, the effect of drugs, etc.

The drawbacks of the method are the monotony of the work as compared with mental work in every-day life, the muscular fatigue sometimes experienced by the unpractised subject, the onset of automaticity, and the difficulty of allowing for the various factors influencing the performance of the task. Taking the last-mentioned difficulty first, we find on analysis the two obvious and opposed factors of practice and fatigue. In addition to this we have irregularities in the amount of work due to sudden 'spurts.' Such spurts are from time to time inevitable; they are especially liable to occur at the start, and when the subject believes the end is nearing. They may even occur whenever the minute signal is given. We have also irregularities of work due to a previous pause. Indeed much care has been expended in finding the relation between say half-an-hour's work done before a rest pause and half-an-hour's work done after that pause. During the pause, the results of fatigue and of practice pass away; but, in addition to the gain and loss of work respectively produced thereby, we have a certain retardation which is due, not so much to mere loss of practice effect, as to the 'growing cold' of the nervous mechanism. There is a certain inertia in starting; the machine needs to be 'warmed up' after each pause, before it can work satisfactorily.

The onset of automaticity is a serious difficulty, which few workers have thought necessary to take

into account. It is extraordinary how entirely independent of the subject's active attention the adding
of figures becomes, when pursued, say for an hour
daily, for a few successive days. The subject's
thoughts soon wander from one topic to another,
while the process of addition continues gaily and
apparently as fast as ever. Attempts have been made
to overcome this difficulty by substituting for addition
the multiplication of three or four consecutive figures
'in the head.' But even this becomes ere long
automatic, the errors throughout being relatively
quite small. The muscular cramp which is sometimes
complained of may be obviated by excusing the
subject from writing down the products of his additions. This procedure, of course, is only possible in
the case of reliable, conscientious individuals.

The monotony of the work cannot be gainsaid.
But as simplicity and uniformity of material are
essential at the start of every scientific enquiry, we
must be content to recognise our limitations and
make the best use of our experiments, before passing to
more complex conditions of experiment, presenting
closer analogy to those of every-day life.

With these drawbacks of the method in mind, we
may pass on to the description of certain experiments
which will show some of the objects of the application
of the test. In these experiments addition or multiplication work is performed for twenty minutes. On

some days the twenty minutes' work is uninterrupted, while on other days a varying period of rest is introduced between the first and the last ten minutes of work. The amount of work done in the first and in the last ten minutes under these different conditions is compared, and it is assumed that the work done on the day of the most favourable length of pause may be used as a basis for estimating the subject's fatigability. Suppose, for an example, the amount of his work is found to be increased by an average of 26·2 per cent. after his most favourable pause, and suppose that, during the first half of the days on which no pause occurred, he performed 370 additions. Then on the second half of the pauseless days we should have expected (had there been a pause so as to get rid of fatigue) an increase of 26·2 per cent. on 370, that is one would have expected a performance of 466 additions. As a matter of fact the subject is found to perform an average of only 437 additions. In other words, there is a loss of 7 per cent. which one may assume to be due mainly to fatigue. Some subjects may show as much as 40 per cent. of loss, others only 2 per cent. according to their fatigability.

Let us now pass to the determination of a subject's retentiveness of improvement due to practice. Suppose a subject performs 445 additions before his most favourable pause and 520 after it. The increase in his work amounts to 16·8 per cent.; wherefore we

8—2

should expect that, if there were no loss of practice, he should perform 16·8 per cent. more additions than 520 (i.e. 607 additions) on the next occasion of his work after a given interval, e.g a day or week. Suppose that he actually performs 564 additions a week later; then the amount representing the loss of practice is 7 per cent. The greater the retentiveness of improvement due to practice, the less, of course, will be the loss.

Neither of these methods for determining fatigability and retentiveness of practice effects is free from objections. But we will waive them and proceed to show the results of examining twelve school boys by these methods, the tasks being the addition of pairs of figures and the multiplication of three figures in the head.

| | Addition | | Multiplication | |
Subject	Fatigability	Retentiveness of practice effects	Fatigability	Retentiveness of practice effects
B	Low	High	Low	High
C	Low	High	Low	High
D	Low	Moderate	Low	High
F	Low	Low	High	Moderate
G	High	Moderate	Low	High
H	Moderate	High	Low	High
L	Moderate	Low	High	Low
M	Fairly high	Moderate	Moderate	Moderate
P	High	Low	High	Low
S	High	Fairly high	High	Low
W	Low	High	High	Low
Y	High	Low	Moderate	Low

For subjects of school age there can be no doubt that the two tasks differ materially in character. It is therefore not surprising that the degree of fatigability or retentiveness is not the same for any one subject in the addition and in the multiplication work. But what does appear very strikingly from the above table is the almost complete inverse relation between fatigability and retentiveness of practice effects. Those boys who best retain their improvement by practice are the least subject to fatigue, while those who are most subject to fatigue show the poorest retention of their gain by practice.

The relation of improvability to retentiveness of improvement by practice has likewise been investigated, and some observers claim to have established the important generalisation that high improvability is associated with low retentiveness and with great fatigability, but this has been disputed in subsequent investigations. It is generally agreed that the total output of work bears no relation to the three factors which we have had here under consideration.

The following data will serve to show the application of the multiplication test to the study of the effects of drugs. On two days no liquid was taken at all, on another day a control mixture was taken, its taste being indistinguishable from the alcohol-containing mixtures which were taken on the five remaining days. The figures give the number of

mental multiplications of four figures (e.g. 4 × 6 × 3 × 8)
performed by the subject in a period of twenty-five
minutes during two intervals between the recording
of ergograms.

	No dose	20 c.c. Alcohol	Control Mixture	40 c.c. Alcohol	No dose	40 c.c. Alcohol	40 c.c. Alcohol	20 c.c. Alcohol
First Interval	659	753	673	698	751	701	736	771
Second Interval	707	735	740	755	766	774	785	780

These data fail to show any striking effect of
alcohol on mental work. The figures during the first
interval are exceedingly irregular; those during the
second interval show a progressive increase due to
practice, and perhaps a larger amount of work with
the strongest doses of alcohol. The calculation of the
number of errors in multiplication throws no light on
any special influence of alcohol.

Further experiments with the larger doses of
alcohol appear to show the same inconstant effects on
arithmetical productivity as on muscular work, in
some cases an increase, in others a decrease or no
difference, being reported. That these irregularities
are real and not due to mere accident is indicated by
the fact that where in recent experiments an effect
upon muscular work in one direction has been shown
on any day, an effect in the same direction on mental
work has also been demonstrated on the same day.

Letter-erasing tests. Several printed sheets of
non-sense words are prepared so that the words prove

of equal difficulty to different individuals. The subject is required to cross out every specimen of a certain letter, e.g. every *e*, which he can find. He reads through the pages line by line, and at the end of every minute a signal is sounded by the experimenter, the subject making a mark at the word at which he has arrived. The test is continued, say for an hour, and the amount of work done is determined by counting the number of *e*'s erased and the number carelessly omitted. The speed, the rate and regularity of improvement from day to day, the number of omissions, the onset of fatigue—and their variations in different individuals or in the same individual under different conditions—can be studied by this method. Like other tests which we have already described, it tends to become automatic owing to its monotonous character.

CHAPTER VII

Tests of free association. A great variety of tests may be devised under this head. Our choice depends on the object we have in view.

To determine the speed with which one word or idea calls forth the next, a stop-watch reading to fifths of seconds is often a sufficiently sensitive instrument for ordinary purposes. Greater exactness may be obtained by the use of more complex electrical apparatus registering thousandth parts of seconds. But such instruments, as a rule, are quite unnecessary. The experimenter has to exhibit the word or object to the subject and at the same time to start the stop-watch ; when the subject replies, the experimenter immediately stops the watch. We have already referred (p. 76) to conditions under which these association times may be of value. They have also been investigated in studying the influence of the age of the subject, drugs, fatigue, education, occupation, and the like. They are easy enough to obtain, but as soon as we attempt to interpret the differences obtained, our difficulties begin. We are dependent entirely on the introspection of the subject. An unusually long association time may in one case mean that an unusually long interval elapsed before any idea occurred to the subject. But the same result may be due to the fact that although a thought was quite distinctly in the mind of the subject, he was nevertheless for some time unable to reply with a word which would put this thought into verbal form. Or the subject may have experienced an extraordinarily rapid flight of thought, so many thoughts occurring to him that it was impossible for him to reply for some time. Owing to these and similar difficulties, association times become less important than the study of the introspective results, and of the nature of the replies given by any one subject under different experimental conditions, or by different subjects under the same experimental conditions.

The following brief account of the investigations made by a well-known French psychologist on his two daughters, *M* and *A*, aged respectively 14½ and 13 years, are of interest in this connexion. The two children had been educated in absolutely the same environment. Nevertheless, the most striking differences between them are brought out by the tests applied.

In one of these tests the subject is told to write down twenty words. A stop-watch is used by the experimenter, but is concealed from the subject. After the twenty words have been written out, the experimenter reads each word aloud and asks the subject what it meant and how it came to be thought of. The children are investigated separately on several occasions, and the entire experiment is repeated after a year's interval with like results. It is found that M writes much more slowly than A, but that she can explain a far greater number of her words than can her younger sister. The average number of unexplainable words is 4·6 per cent. for M, 28 per cent. for A. This is partly ascribable to the difference of speed of writing, for when M is pressed to write more rapidly, her proportion of unexplained words rises enormously; this is likewise the case with A.

But the difference is also due to the fact that M has the better memory, that she is less liable to distraction, that her thoughts are more definite, and that she is more inclined to attend to meaning than to mere verbalism. The number of words referring to objects surrounding the subject is far greater (37·5 per cent.) in the case of M than in the case of A (10 per cent.), suggesting that A is richer in ideas than M who, on the other hand, is a closer observer of the outer world. So too the words used by M are found to refer more often to her own person. Such words are extremely rare in A ; in M they amount to about 5 per cent. Again, M writes much more frequently (53·7 per cent.) of past experiences than does her younger sister. The difference is not so much due to memory as to interest, for of A's recollections 64 per cent. are more than three months' old, while in M such recollections only reach 25 per cent. The same cause is indicated by the fact that while A is particularly fond of cycling, she hardly ever alludes to it in her words, while M frequently does so.

Equally striking are the differences in frequency of words involving abstract ideas. With M they all occur during the first five sittings and none later,— 3·7 per cent. in all. With A they amount to 23·3 per cent. If each girl determines to write down the objects within a house, M chooses her own house, while A chooses any house,—houses in general. A often writes down words without understanding their meaning ; she shows instances of 'verbal' association —passing from one word to another (e.g. from *case* to *race*) merely through the likeness of sound—more often than does her elder sister. M never constructs fictitious scenes, while A occasionally (7·6 per cent.) does so. A's images are poor in detail, but that does not prevent her, when writing 'carriage,' from thinking of one overturned near a bridge,—a scene which she subsequently declares to be imaginary,—nor when writing 'butterfly' from thinking of a wood which she insists she has never visited and of a coloured butterfly which she has never actually seen.

It is obvious that A is decidedly the more 'original' child. While M runs with monotonous regularity through series of objects of the same character, A passes rapidly from one theme to the other. In contrast to her sister, A shows few associations of contiguity. Her associations are formal, logical, or are due to similarity of meaning. She does not run through an obvious series of associations; hers is a much more complex procedure, resulting in original, zig-zag lines of thought. Thus the two children may be said to speak a different language, owing to differences in the form of their intelligence. M's better memory (as shown in other experiments), her special predilection for recalling recent events, the precision of her observations, her attachment to objects of the external world,—all are in striking contrast to the abstract thought of A, which gives her a far more technical and refined vocabulary, including words as to whose meaning she is extremely vague.

We may bring this series of contrasting differences to a close by giving an account of the independent descriptions by the two sisters of two common objects placed before them.

The first is—A leaf of a chestnut tree.

M's essay, written in 11 minutes 15 seconds, is as follows:—

'The leaf I see before me comes from the chestnut tree. It was gathered in autumn, for almost all the leaflets (save two) are yellow, and one is half green and yellow.

This is a leaf composed of seven leaflets, uniting at a centre which ends in the stalk called the petiole; and this attaches the leaf to the tree.

Not all the leaflets are of the same size: four of the seven are much smaller than the other three.

The chestnut is a dicotyledon; one can see that from the ramifying venation of the leaf.

In several parts the leaf is dotted with spots of rust colour, there is a hole in one of the leaflets.

I do not know what more to say about this chestnut leaf.'

A's essay, written in 8 minutes, is as follows:—

'This is the leaf of a chestnut tree, which has only lately fallen, withered before the winds of autumn.

The leaf is yellow, but it is still stiff and uncurled. Perhaps a little strength yet remains in the poor thing.

The leaves still bear some traces of their former green colour, but yellow is the prevailing tone. Their edges bear a brown and reddish streak.

The seven leaves are all still very beautiful; the greenish stalk is not yet separated from them.

Poor leaf, now destined to take wing upon the roads, there to decay amid a heap of many others. It is dead to-day...it lived yesterday. Yesterday, hanging from the branch, it awaited the fatal gust of wind which should detach it,—as one on his death-bed who awaits his last agony. But the leaf was unaware of its danger. It fell placidly to the ground.'

The theme of the second essay is—A French halfpenny (*sou*).

M's essay, written in 5½ minutes :—

'The coin before me is a *sou*; it is made of copper and is worn through long use. One side of this coin shows an eagle with spread wings, for it dates from the Emperor Napoleon III. On this side is written—'Empire Français, 5 centimes.'

On the reverse side is the head of Napoleon III., surrounded by the words 'Napoléon Empereur' and, below, the year when the coin was issued, but it is so worn that I cannot read it.

This coin is thin; it is about two millimetres thick.'

A's essay, written in 6 minutes :—

'It is an old *sou* worn by time. The head of Napoleon III. is still distinguishable on the darker dirty background. Some spots of verdigris occur about the words 'Napoleon III., emperor,' and then comes the date. On the other side of the coin the letters are more worn, and hardly anything can now be made out. What a long story this *sou* could tell, if only it could speak ! Where has it come from ? Into whose hands has it fallen ?

But there ! We ought not to have such thoughts, when looking at a lowly little coin like a *sou* ; we should not seek its history. Oh no ! To behold a *sou* seems such a simple common thing. *Sous* pass unheeded like many objects we are accustomed to meet with everywhere.'

These and other tests show very clearly how different are the minds of the two sisters. The elder contents herself with a precise description of detail, a kind of inventory of the object under examination. The younger sister makes up in imagination, in unity of design and in literary skill what she lacks in precision and observation. She is often inaccurate or careless in details, and these details are always subordinate to an impression of unity of purpose, often to a sentiment, which runs through the whole.

A year later these tests of description of an object were repeated. *M*'s characteristics persisted unaltered. *A*, on the other hand, showed a marked change. She was content to describe the object like her sister, but less minutely and accurately. The experimenter, astonished at this change, then showed her her former description, and received the reply, 'I don't care to write that sort of thing now,—it seems silly.'

The standardisation of intelligence. The following tests have been successfully used in an examination
of some 200 French school-children, ranging from three
to twelve years of age, in infant and primary public
schools. Not all the tests then employed are here
given, and the changes which have been made to
adapt them to English conditions are unquestionably
very inadequate. But they will serve to indicate
what may be expected from the application of
correspondingly suitable tests in this country.

One must recognise at the outset the impossibility
of arriving at the standard of a child's intelligence by
a single test. The examiner has to apply several
tests each of a different nature, and he has to judge,
by certain conventional rules hereafter given, whether
the child has reached the average level, or standard,
of intelligence of his age, or whether he is one, two,
or more years in advance of or behind this level or
standard. The tests should include not only those
which depend in great part on school education and
social environment, but also such as are little subject
to these influences and therefore afford a more adequate test of pure intelligence.

I.   Three years of age.

(1)   'Point to your nose,' eyes, mouth, etc.

(2)   Repeat a sentence of six syllables, e.g. 'Let
us go for a walk.'

(3) Repeat two numbers (non-consecutive), e.g. three, seven, slowly pronounced, and separated by a half-second's interval.

(4) 'What is that?' The child is successively presented with three pictures and is expected to describe them. Each picture contains people and certain objects of interest with which he is known to be familiar. [At this age the child should have reached the stage of recognising, identifying, and enumerating objects. Only at the level of 7 years of age does description begin. At 12 interpretation enters, the child usually showing signs of sympathy and the like.]

(5) 'What is your surname?'

II. Four years of age.

(1) 'Are you a little boy or a little girl?'

(2) 'What is this?' asking the child to name a knife, a key or a penny.

(3) Repeat three figures [spoken as in I (3)].

(4) 'You see these lines' (one line of 5 cms., the other of 6 cms., parallel to one another and separated by a distance of 3 cms.[1]). 'Tell me which is the longer.'

III. Five years of age.

(1) Repeat a sentence of twelve syllables.

(2) 'You see these two boxes. Tell me which is

[1] See footnote on p. 33 for corresponding British measure.

the heavier.' The two boxes are of the same shape and size, the weight of one being 3 grams[1], the other 12 grams. They are placed on the table before the child, a distance of 5—6 cms. being left between them.

(3) 'Copy this square.' The child is given a fountain pen to draw with. The square shown him has sides of about 3 cms.

(4) 'You see these pennies. Count them. Tell me how many there are.' Four pennies are placed on a table juxtaposed. The experimenter insists on the child counting. (A Parisian) child of 3 cannot count four pennies. At 4 half the children succeed. At 5 only the backward fail.

(5) 'Put these two cards together so that they make a figure like that.' Two oblongs of the same size are cut out of cardboard. One of these is left whole and serves as the copy, the other is divided diagonally, so as to form two triangles. The oblong card is placed on a table before the child, and the two triangular pieces are so placed before him that their hypotenuses are as far distant from one another as possible. Only a third of the children tested succeed at 4 years old ; hardly one in twelve fails at 5 years.

IV.   Six years of age.

(1)   Repeat a sentence of sixteen words. Half the children succeed at 5, all at 6 years of age.

[1] See footnote on p. 33 for corresponding British measure.

(2) 'Which is the prettier of these two drawings?' Drawings of six faces have been prepared, three ugly, three beautiful, and the three pairs of drawings are successively shown to the child.

(3) 'What is a fork?' (a table, chair, horse, etc.). Five objects are set for definition, and the preponderating characteristics of the definitions are noted. At 4 years old half the children define by mere usage (e.g., a horse is for drawing carriages), at 6 all the children can do so. At 9 most children give definitions of a higher order (e.g., the horse is an animal that draws carriages).

(4) 'You see this key. Go and put it on that chair over there. Next, shut the door. Then you will notice a box which is on a chair near the door. Bring me that box. So, first put the key on the chair, then shut the door, and then bring me the box. You understand? Now then, be off!' Here three directions have to be carried out in prescribed order. At 4 years of age hardly any child succeeds, at 5 half succeed, at 6 all or nearly all.

(5) 'What is your age?' Most children do not know their age before they are 6 years old.

V. Seven years of age.

(1) 'What is missing in this drawing?' A face is shown lacking an eye, a mouth or nose, or a full length figure is shown lacking arms.

(2) 'How many fingers have you on your right hand?' 'How many on your left hand?' 'How many altogether on both hands?'

(3) 'Copy these words.' The child is given pen and ink. The copy consists of three words, 'My little John,' with capitals for the first and last words.

(4) Repeat five figures, spoken as in I (3).

(5) Describe a drawing as in I (4).

VI.   Eight years of age.

(1) Read the following paragraph :—

THREE HOUSES ON FIRE.

Newcastle-on-Tyne, September 5th.   Last night in Newcastle an enormous fire destroyed three houses situated in the centre of the town.   Seventeen families are now homeless.   The damage exceeds £6000.   A young barber was seriously burnt about the hands in rescuing an infant from its cradle.

The observer notes the time taken to read these 53 words.   The average time for (Parisian) children of

$$8 \text{ years is found to be } 45 \text{ seconds}$$

9	,,	,,	,,	,,	,,	40	,,
10	,,	,,	,,	,,	,,	30	,,
11	,,	,,	,,	,,	,,	25	,,

The observer should look out for the following characteristic defects in reading.   Does the child spell the words, does he pause between each syllable,

does he pause between the words, does he misread or
mispronounce any words, does he halt only at marks
of punctuation, does he read expressively or in a
monotone? After a pause of two or three seconds,
the examiner says to the child 'Now tell me what
you have just been reading.' Some persuasion may be
necessary, but it should not be continued for longer
than ten seconds. The examiner writes down exactly
what the child replies, and then counts the number
of facts remembered. The maximum number is
nineteen, and is reckoned as follows, the words in
brackets which occur twice being excluded.

Three. Houses. On fire. Newcastle-on-Tyne.
September 5th. Last night. (In Newcastle) an enormous fire. Destroyed (three houses). Situated in
the centre of the town. Seventeen families. Are
now homeless. The damage exceeds £6000. A
young barber. Was seriously. Burnt. About the
hands. In rescuing. An infant. From its cradle.

(2) 'What are these colours?' asks the examiner,
pointing with his finger successively to four oblong
patches of coloured paper, each measuring 6 × 2 cms.
all mounted on a single piece of cardboard. Familiar
colours (red, yellow, blue, green) are chosen.

(3) 'Count from 20 backwards,—20, 19, and
so on.'

(4) 'Write down these words.' Quite a short
phrase, e.g., 'the pretty little birds,' is read by the

examiner. At 7 only a third of the children are able to write from dictation, at 8 all can do so.

(5) 'You know what butterflies are, you have seen them, haven't you?' 'Yes.' 'And you know what bees are also?' 'Yes.' 'Is a butterfly the same as a bee?' 'No.' 'What is the difference between them?' At 6 a third of the children make comparisons, at 7 almost all, at 8 all.

VII.   Nine years.

(1) 'What is the day of the week?' 'What is this month?' 'What is the day of the month?' 'What is this year?' A little latitude in the day of the month may be allowed. Most children cannot answer these questions satisfactorily until they are 9 years old. In one school, composed of much younger children, where it had been long the custom for each child at the close of each day's lessons to recite answers to these questions, not a single child was able to give a complete answer to the test. This shows the folly of teaching children prematurely.

(2) 'What are the names of the days of the week? Tell me them in order.' This must be done without hesitation or error in ten seconds.

(3) The same kind of reading test is given as in VI (1). At 8 all children are able to read aloud, but hardly any can recollect six facts from this particular reading test, which is undeniably difficult

at this age ; their attention is too closely concentrated on the matter, and is not free to be directed to the sense. At 9, on the other hand, nearly all children can remember six facts.

(4) 'These five boxes are not all of the same weight. Some are heavy, others are light. I want you to place them in order, putting the heaviest here, the next heaviest here, the next here, and so on down to the lightest, which you will place here.' During these instructions the examiner points on the table to the positions in which the boxes are to be severally arranged. The weights are small boxes of cardboard of exactly the same form, size and colour, but weighing 3, 6, 9, 12, 15 grams respectively.

(5) Test power of definition, see IV (3).

VIII. Ten years.

(1) 'Tell me the months of the year in order.' One month forgotten or misplaced may be allowed. Otherwise there should be no difficulty or hesitation ; the time taken should not exceed 15 seconds.

(2) 'Give me the names of these coins ; do not touch them.' A halfpenny, penny, threepenny-piece, sixpence, shilling, florin, half-crown, half-sovereign, sovereign, are placed on the table in irregular order, and the examiner points to each in turn.

(3) 'Write a single short sentence containing

these three words.' The instructions may be repeated several times, if they are not understood. The words 'London, money, gutter' will serve as an example. One minute is allowed for writing. Unless most of it is completed by then, the child is reckoned to have failed. The results afford a good measure of the intellectual level of the child. At the lowest stage he writes down three distinct thoughts, e.g., 'London is a big city, money is to buy things with, a gutter takes away the water at the side of the road.' When still more advanced, he expresses two thoughts: 'In London, there are gutters, and there are men who have made much money.' Such a stage is never reached at 7 years, rarely at 8, by about a third of the children at 9, and by half at 10. In the highest stage, a single phrase is written, e.g., 'I found some money in a gutter in London,' or the phrases, though distinct, are very closely connected, e.g., 'I live in London ; in my street there is a gutter to drain the water away ; a little way from my father's house, lives a gentleman I know, who has a great deal of money.' At 10 one quarter succeed in writing the words in one sentence.

(4) To test ability to understand. Examples with replies: 'What ought one to do when one has missed one's train ?' Good reply: 'Wait for the next.' Bad replies: 'Run after it,' 'Buy a ticket.'

'When you have broken something that does not belong to you, what should you do?' Good replies : 'Pay for it,' 'Apologize.' Bad replies: 'I should cry,' 'I should go to the police-station.' Three questions are asked, two good answers suffice. At 7 or 8 half the children reply satisfactorily, at 9 three quarters, at 10 all.

(5) A second series of five questions, involving greater difficulty, may then be set, e.g., 'What ought you to do, when you find you are starting late for school?' 'Why are you more disposed to forgive a person for injuring you if he was angry at the moment, than if he was not angry?' 'Why should a man be judged by his deeds rather than by his words?' The examiner must naturally be patient in applying this test. Two bad answers in five may be passed. At 7 or 8, children never give good answers to these harder questions, at 10 barely half reply satisfactorily. Thus the test may be said to mark the transition between 10 and 11 years of age.

IX. Eleven years of age.

(1) 'I am going to read you sentences in each of which there is something ridiculous. Listen carefully, and tell me whenever you find anything silly.' The examiner reads each sentence slowly in a tone of

uniform conviction and then, at once changing his
tone, asks 'What is there silly in that?' Example
and replies : 'An unfortunate cyclist had his skull
fractured and he died on the spot. He was brought
to the hospital, but no hope is entertained of his
recovery.' Good reply : 'If he were dead, he could
not recover.' Bad replies : 'It is silly to go bicycling,'
'There is nothing silly in it.' Other examples:'I have
three brothers, John, William and myself.' 'There
was a railway accident yesterday, but it was not
serious. The number of deaths was only 48.' Five
tests are given, of which at least three should be
solved. At 9 hardly a single child succeeds, at 10
scarcely a quarter of the children, at 11 a half.

(2) 'Give me as many words as you can in three
minutes, words like table, beard, shirt, carriage.' The
spirit of competition is roused by telling the child
that some of his school-fellows have given more than
200 words in three minutes. The results of this test
must be considered in relation to our previous re-
marks on pp. 122, 123. No test can be termed successful unless at least 60 words are given. This is
reached at 11 years, but occasionally the number may
exceed 200.

(3) 'What do you mean by charity, justice,
kindness?' These words are successively given ; two
good definitions should be obtained. At 11 most
children succeed, at 10 a third. Occasional successes

are met with in children of 8 or 9. Good definitions: 'Kindness is returning good for evil.' 'Charity is giving money to the old who can no longer work.' Bad definitions: 'Justice is judgment,' 'Kindness is to be well dressed.'

(4) The test of VIII (3) is repeated. All normal children of 11 succeed in writing the three words in one sentence.

(5) 'Put these words in such order that they make sense.'

Examples   (i)   To Asked Spelling
                     My I Master
                     Correct My.
         (ii)   A Bravely
                     Dog Good His
                     Master Defends.

Three tests are given. Each should be solved within one minute, or it is counted a failure. The child must succeed in two of the three tests in order to pass.

X.   Twelve years of age.

(1) A child should be able to reproduce sentences of 26 syllables without a mistake. The following which are read by the examiner will serve as specimens.

24 syllables:—' We all have to work hard in order

to live. Every morning you ought therefore to go to school.'

26 syllables 'The other day I saw a lovely brown dog in the street Little Harry has dirtied his new pinafore.'

28   „   'John is often punished for his naughtiness. I bought a beautiful doll at a toy-shop for my little sister.'

30   „   'Last night there was a terrible storm with much lightning. Frederick has caught a cold, he is feverish and has a bad cough.'

(2) 'Do you know what a rhyme is?' Whether the child knows or not, the examiner explains, 'Two words rhyme when they end in the same way. For instance *mention* rhymes with *intention* because both end in *ention*. *Enjoys* rhymes with *employs* because both end with *oys*. You understand? Now I am going to give you a word and you are to find a lot of other words which rhyme with it. The word is drawn. Give me all the words that rhyme with drawn.' One minute is allowed, by the end of which the child should have found three rhymes. The examiner should stimulate him, but must not otherwise help him.

(3) Repeat 7 numbers as in I (3). The child is warned that there will be 7 numbers to repeat. He is allowed three trials, in which one success is enough.

(4) Test ability to interpret. Two sentences are read and good answers should be obtained to both of them. The following is an example :—
'My neighbour has just been receiving some unusual visitors. First came a doctor, then a lawyer, and then a clergyman. What can have happened in his house?' Good answer: 'He is very ill, he is dying,' 'Someone in his house is very ill, he is dead.' Bad answers 'I do not know,' 'He has been visited by a doctor and a clergyman.'

(5) To describe a drawing as in I (4).

It is impossible to measure intelligence as we measure stature. We cannot take the result of a single test and place the child according to his position with reference to the average result which a child of his age is known to reach. It will often happen that a child fails in one test yet succeeds in all the others which he ought to be able to do at his age. We must hence allow a failure in one test, if he reaches the standard in the rest. Thus, if a child fulfils all the tests save one for seven years, and proceeds to fulfil all the tests save one for eight years, we conclude that his intelligence reaches the level of an eight years' old child.

Another convention is also desirable. Suppose

a child of eight succeeds in all the tests of his year save two, and all the tests of the ninth year save two, we cannot justly say that he has only reached the level of a seven year child. We should be disregarding the three tests at eight and the three at nine which he has successfully performed. We say that he has performed six tests of an age higher than seven years. We allow any number of such higher tests, exceeding four and less than nine, to count as one year, and ten such tests to count as two years. Consequently the child is said to have reached a level of eight years.

The question arises whether a child who fails to pass the tests of its own age ever succeeds in passing those of a higher age. No such case occurred among 70 French children specially tested for this purpose, but possibly owing to the unsuitable nature of some of these tests for this country, this may occur here.

The following table shows the number of children among 192 who are at the level of, in advance of, and behind, the standards here laid down.

	Years										Total
	3	4	5	6	7	8	9	10	11	12	
At the mean level ...	3	9	13	5	7	16	11	14	13	2	93
One year in advance	3	2	6	8	7	5	9	2	—	—	42
Two years in advance	—	1	—	—	—	1	—	—	—	—	2
One year behind ...	4	4	4	6	3	1	2	9	5	5	43
Two years behind ...	—	1	—	1	1	—	—	3	2	4	12

That is to say, the number of normal children is

approximately equal to the number of those who are in advance of or behind the normal. The small number of children—only 14—who are two years in advance of or behind the standard is another striking proof of the success of the scheme[1].

There are one or two less satisfactory features. The relatively great number of backward children at 3 and 4 years of age is perhaps due in great part to shyness, or to wilful error. The large number of backward children of 10 years (almost equal to the number of normal children of nine years) suggests some defect in the tests which may be remedied with further experience.

It has been suggested that a child who is materially behind the standard may be classed as backward, as an imbecile, or as an idiot, according to the level which he is found to reach. The tests, repeated from time to time, will usefully show the extent to which the intelligence of the defective child improves or deteriorates with educational or medical treatment. The well-known beneficial effect of thyroid extract on the backward intelligence of 'cretins' may be tested by this means.

In this and the preceding chapters we have

[1] The memoir, from which this table is taken, states that 203 children were investigated, that 103 were at the mean level and that 44 were a year behind. The data, however, which are given for the various years of age, necessitate the above modification of this statement.

already indicated several uses to which 'mental' tests have been or may be put. We have seen how they may be employed in studying the differences between individuals and between communities, and in investigating the effect of drugs. We have seen too how they may be turned to account in determining the grade of intelligence in a given individual. We conclude this chapter by calling attention to other investigations in which these tests have played a part

One such investigation has for its object the determination of sex differences. A convenient way of evaluating the results is to take the individual results yielded, say, by the female sex, to arrange them in order of magnitude and to take the middle value, the 'median' as it is technically called, as expressing the mean of that series. We then find out what percentage of the male sex gives results equal or superior to the median of the females. The opposite table gives this percentage for different tests. They must be regarded rather as an illustration of method than as strictly comparable and reliable data.

A and B consist of University students, C and D of Elementary, E and F of High school children.

Generally speaking, these and other differences thus obtained are but slight. The median values for the two sexes are closely similar. The male sex appears to be slightly inferior to the female in sensibility and in immediate memory, and slightly to excel in control over movement and in solving puzzles that call for ingenuity. One may at first sight be satisfied with attributing such differences to the influence of previous training, but this explanation is only superficial, inasmuch as the differences of training are determined by innate differences in mental constitution.

	A	B	C	D	E	F
Reaction time	68	81	57	—	76	—
Rate of tapping	81	60	64	—	73	—
Discrimination of pitch	44	40	—	—	—	
Letter erasing test	—	32	—	33	—	
Immediate memory for nonsense syllables heard	32	—	—	—	—	—
Immediate memory for nonsense syllables read	46	—	—	—	—	—
Memory, after 10—30″, for words	—	—	—	40	—	—
Addition, multiplication and like tests	—	—	—	48	—	50

A more significant difference comes to light when instead of comparing the values of the median in the two sexes, we enquire into the extent to which individuals of either sex diverge from their respective medians. The evidence shows that males are much more variable than the females. The averages may not be noticeably different, but the number of abnormally superior and inferior persons and the degree of superiority and inferiority attained are greater in the male than in the female. These results are in agreement with the familiar fact that genius and insanity are of commoner occurrence among men than among women.

Another line of investigation has for its object the discovery of unit mental characters or functions. The old method of representing these units as a small number of broad 'faculties,' the faculty of memory, of reasoning, and the like, has fallen into such disrepute that the notion of faculty dare hardly be used by the psychologist who has a reputation to uphold for respectability. We know now that the faculty, say of mathematical ability, is not a single unit, but that it involves a multitude of unit functions, which are by no means correlated.

Suitable statistical methods allow us to determine numerically the extent to which such mental characters or functions are correlated. When the correlation is such that excellence of an individual in one character is always found to involve corresponding excellence in another character, the order of persons excelling in one being the same as the order of excellence in the other character, the coefficient of correlation has the value + 1. When the correlation is as uniformly inverse, the order of excellence for the one character being exactly reversed in the order of excellence for the other, the coefficient has the value − 1. And between these the coefficient has every value according to the degree of direct or inverse correlation, passing through zero when there is no correlation whatever.

We have called attention (p. 117) to a striking instance of inverse correlation,—between fatigability and retention of improvement in certain mental work. We have just now stated that the correlation between different branches of mathematics is by no means great ; a study of correlation has shown, for example, that there is hardly any correlation at all in schools between proficiency in algebra and proficiency in geometry.

Where correlation between two characters exists, we may assume the presence of some one or more simple factors by which the two characters are influenced in common. Thus we are on the road to discover the unit mental characters of our goal. But the path is comparatively new and the difficulties in the way are enormous ; it is therefore not surprising that the results obtained by different observers are contradictory. The greatest difficulty perhaps consists in the determination of the nature of the unit or units responsible for the correlation obtained. The correlation coefficient can only give a blurred picture of the multitudinous influences which are at work, the dissection and enumeration of which must prove a well nigh insuperable task.

At all events this is a more promising line of investigation than the older one which had for its object the classification of individuals under different types. That kind of work, though far from dead, is fast falling into discredit. It selects extreme cases, extreme cases of vividness (or absence) of visual imagery, extreme cases of development (or lack) of musical ability, and the like—and calls them types. It is based on the popular notion that mankind can be sharply separated into so many classes or species corresponding to these types. But there is no evidence in favour of the view that any community contains distinctly different species of individuals. We do not find gaps between extremely vivid imagery and its absence, between extreme musical ability and its absence, or between the idiot, the normal, and the genius. So far as we can see, mental variations are as a rule continuous; the intermediate conditions are indeed far commoner than the extreme types. Hence if we must have a type theory, it seems better to adopt the view that the human mental type is a single one, like human stature, human fecundity and the like, and to describe any individual as departing to such and such an extent from this single type. It may well be that this continuity of variation is only apparent. It may well be that one day we shall be able to discover a number of units underlying and determining this seeming continuity of mental variation. Now and again our hopes of this end are raised by the discovery of abrupt mental abnormalities, e.g., the two varieties of red-green blindness, between which no intermediate conditions are to be found. But these cases are most exceptional.

Many of the tests which we have been describing serve as indications of innate ability. It is interesting therefore to compare the results of the same tests applied by the same observers in a good Elementary school and in a good Preparatory school of a University town. In all the tests except two—the discrimination of differences of weight and spatial threshold—the average performances of the boys of the Preparatory school were the better. When the boys were ranged according to the order of their intelligence imputed to them by their masters and their school-fellows, these two tests were the only ones which yielded negative correlations with intelligence. All the rest showed positive correlations to a varying extent with the order of intelligence thus determined. These two tests, it will be remembered, are just those which primitive people achieve with greater success than civilised. There is thus good reason to believe from these tests that the boys of superior parentage are of superior intelligence to those of inferior parentage. It may be urged that in certain tests, e.g., those of memory, the Preparatory school boys were specially favoured by previous training. But in familiarity with music this was certainly not the case, and as regards previous manual training the Elementary school children might have been expected to succeed better in the motor section of the tests than the Preparatory school children.   Nor can it be maintained that conditions of nourishment and home environment played an important part in determining the differences, as the parents of the boys at the Elementary school were able to afford a weekly fee of ninepence. The most striking contrast between the two schools consisted in the different level of general mental ability in the parentage.

It is interesting, too, to observe that the same tests, repeated eighteen months later on the same boys of the Elementary school, showed very little change in the capacities tested, despite the fact that in the interval the progress of their knowledge had in many cases been considerable and the interests of the boys had so altered that their class order was very different.   This is a further indication of the value of such tests for determining innate abilities.   Indeed no one can apply these simple tests without being struck with the wealth of information any one of them yields in regard to the subject's mental capacity.

BIBLIOGRAPHY

CHAPTER I

Helmholtz, H. von. Handbuch der physiologischen Optik, Hamburg u. Leipzig, 1909—(new edition in course of publication).

Hering, E. Grundzüge der Lehre vom Lichtsinn, Leipzig, 1905—(in course of publication).

McDougall, W. "Some New Observations in support of Thomas Young's Theory of Light and Colour Vision," Mind, 1901 (N.S.), x, 52, 210, 347 ; "An Investigation of the Colour Sense of Two Infants," Brit. Journ. of Psychology, 1908, II, 338.

Myers, C. S. "Some Observations on the Development of the Colour Sense," ibid., 353.

Rivers, W. H. R. "Primitive Colour Vision," Popular Science Monthly, LIX, 44-58 ; "Observations on the Senses of the Todas," Brit. Journ. of Psychol., 1905, I, 326-339.

Smith, E. M. "Some Observations concerning Colour Vision in Dogs," ibid., 1912, v, 119-202.

Valentine, C. W. "The Colour Perception and Colour Preferences of an Infant during its Fourth and Eighth Months," ibid., 1914, VI, 363-386.

Washburn, M. F. The Animal Mind, New York, 1908.

CHAPTER II

Rivers, W. H. R. and Head, H. "A Human Experiment in Nerve Division," Brain, 1908, XXXI, 323-450, where a useful bibliography is given.

BIBLIOGRAPHY

CHAPTER III

Judd, C. H., McAllister, C. N. and Steele, W. M. "Introduction to a Series of Studies of Eye Movements by means of Kinetoscopic Photographs," Psychological Review, Monograph Supplements, 1905, VII, No. 1.

Lewis, E. O. "The Effect of Practice on the Müller-Lyer Illusions," Brit. Journ. of Psychol., 1908, II, 294; "Confluxion and Contrast Effects in the Müller-Lyer Illusion," ibid., 1909, III, 21.

Rivers, W. H. R. Reports of the Cambridge Anthropological Expedition to the Torres Straits, Cambridge, 1901, II, Part I, 97; "Observations on the Senses of the Todas," Brit. Journ. of Psychol., 1905, I, 356.

CHAPTER IV

Bullough, E. "The 'Perceptive Problem' in the Aesthetic Appreciation of Single Colours," Brit. Journ. of Psychol., 1908, II, 406; "The 'Perceptive Problem' in the Aesthetic Appreciation of Single Colour Combinations," ibid., 1910, III, 406.

Külpe, O. "Der gegenwärtige Stand der experimentellen Ästhetik," Berichte d. II Kongress f. exp. Psychol., Leipzig, 1907, 1.

Myers, C. S. "A Study of Rhythm in Primitive Music," Brit. Journ. of Psychol., 1905, I, 397; "The Ethnological Study of Music," Anthropological Essays presented to Edward Burnett Tylor, Oxford, 1907, 235.

Valentine, C. W. An Introduction to the Experimental Psychology of Beauty, London, N.D.

CHAPTER V

Myers, C. S. A Text book of Experimental Psychology (chapters 12 and 13), 2nd edition, Cambridge, 1911.

CHAPTERS VI AND VII

Binet, A. L'Étude expérimentale de l'Intelligence, Paris, 1903.

Binet, A. et Simon, Th. "Le Développement de l'Intelligence," L'Année Psychologique, 14ᵐᵉ Année, 1908, 1.

Brown, W. Mental Measurement, Cambridge, 1911.

Burt, C. "Experimental Tests of General Intelligence," Brit. Journ. of Psychol., 1909, III, 94.

McDougall, W. Reports of the Cambridge Anthropological Expedition to Torres Straits, Cambridge, 1903, II, Pt. II, 189.

Myers, C. S. Ibid., 155.

Rivers, W. H. R. Ibid., 1901, II, Part I, 12; "Observations on the Senses of the Todas," op. cit., 323; The Influence of Alcohol and other Drugs on Fatigue, London, 1908.

Spearman, C. "General Intelligence Objectively Determined and Measured," Amer. Journ. of Psychol., 1904, xv, 201.

Thorndike, E. L. Educational Psychology, 2nd edition, New York, 1910.

Whipple, G. M. Manual of Mental and Physical Tests, Baltimore, 1910.

Wimms, J. H. "The Relative Effects of Fatigue and Practice produced by Different Kinds of Mental Work," Brit. Journ. of Psychol., 1907, I, 153.

INDEX

www.ingramcontent.com/pod-product-compliance
Ingram Content Group UK Ltd.
Pitfield, Milton Keynes, MK11 3LW, UK
UKHW042144280225
455719UK00001B/88